This book belongs to

....

PIE
This is not
sign
language
THEATRE

The PASSAGE of TIME
WORD
USWARD
DERN
WELKIN
THESAURUS

Also by Ursula Dubosarsky & Tohby Riddle

The Word Spy
The Word Spy Activity Book

Also by Ursula Dubosarsky

NOVELS

The Red Shoe

Theodora's Gift

Abyssinia

How to be a Great Detective

My Father is not a Comedian!

Black Sails, White Sails

Zizzy Zing

Bruno and the Crumhorn

The First Book of Samuel

The White Guinea Pig

The Last Week in December

High Hopes

The Golden Day

PICTURE BOOKS

Rex
Illustrated by David Mackintosh

Honey and Bear
Illustrated by Ron Brooks

Special Days with Honey and Bear
Illustrated by Ron Brooks

The Terrible Plop
Illustrated by Andrew Joyner

The Carousel
Illustrated by Walter Di Qual

Too Many Elephants in this House!
Illustrated by Andrew Joyner

Also by Tohby Riddle

NOVELS

The Lucky Ones

CARTOON COLLECTIONS

What's the Big Idea?
Pink Freud

PICTURE BOOKS

My Uncle's Donkey

Nobody Owns the Moon

Irving the Magician

The Great Escape from City Zoo

The Singing Hat

The Tip at the End of the Street

The Royal Guest

Arnold Z Jones Could Really Play the Trumpet

A Most Unusual Dog

Careful with that Ball, Eugene!

Dog and Bird and the Caterpillar

Dog and Bird See the Moon

Dog and Bird Follow a Butterfly

Dog and Bird Water the Garden

Unforgotten

Tohby Riddle is a picture book creator, cartoonist and novelist. He has won numerous literary and design awards for his work, and his cartoons have been shown at the National Museum of Australia and feature in a permanent exhibit at the Melbourne Museum. Tohby leapt at the chance to picture The Word Spy's incredible new adventure.

tohby.com

Ursula Dubosarsky was born in Sydney, the third child in a family of writers. She wanted to be a writer from the age of six, and is now the internationally acclaimed author of many books for children. She has won several prestigious literary awards, and has a PhD in English literature from Macquarie University. Ursula is very excited to see The Word Spy back on another amazing wordy quest!

ursuladubosarsky.com

Ursula Dubosarsky

Illustrated by Tohby Riddle

PUFFIN BOOKS

PUFFIN BOOKS

UK | USA | Canada | Ireland | Australia
India | New Zealand | South Africa | China

Penguin Books is part of the Penguin Random House group of companies
whose addresses can be found at global.penguinrandomhouse.com.

First published by Penguin Random House Australia Pty Ltd, 2010
This revised edition published by Penguin Random House Australia Pty Ltd, 2017

1 3 5 7 9 10 8 6 4 2

Cover and text design by Adam Laszcuzuk © Penguin Random House Australia Pty Ltd
Typeset in 12/16pt Adobe Caslon
Colour separation by Splitting Image Colour Studio, Clayton, Victoria
Printed and bound in Australia by Griffin Press, an accredited ISO AS/NZS
14001 Environmental Management Systems printer

National Library of Australia
Cataloguing-in-Publication data:

ISBN 978 0 14 378759 4

With thanks to Peter Le for his assistance with the braille page

penguin.com.au

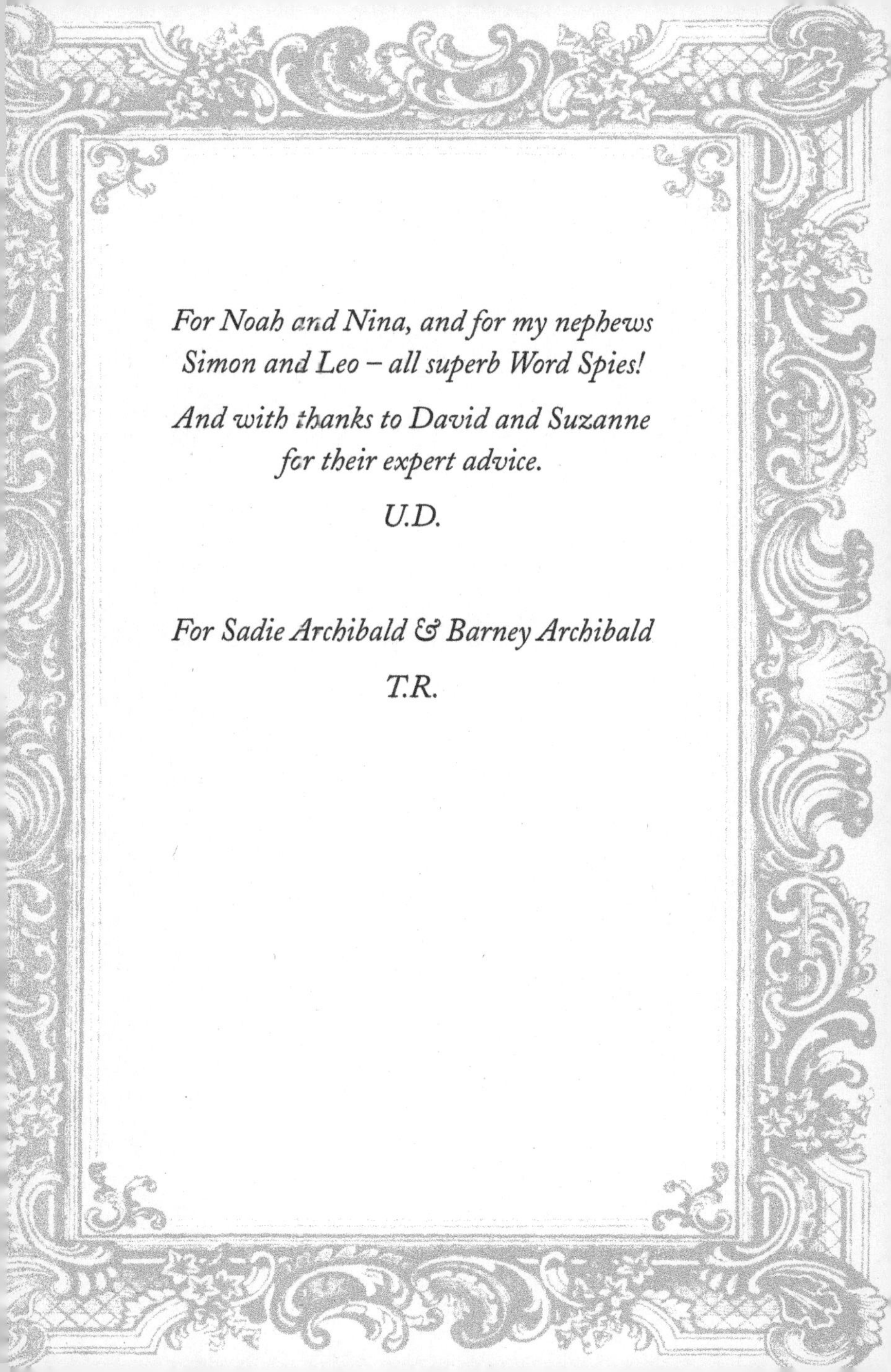

For Noah and Nina, and for my nephews Simon and Leo – all superb Word Spies!

And with thanks to David and Suzanne for their expert advice.

U.D.

For Sadie Archibald & Barney Archibald

T.R.

'To follow knowledge, like a sinking star,
Beyond the utmost bound of human thought.'

Alfred, Lord Tennyson, 'Ulysses'

Dear Word Spies, far and near,

I'm back!

Yes, I've returned. I've galloped, I've hopped, I've swum, I've flown. By foot, by pony, by bus, by plane and train. And here I am at last.

Now, my Spies, there's a reason I've come back. Are you all alone? Yes? Good. Then listen carefully.

When we last met, in my first book The Word Spy, we wandered together round the wonderful world of words. I loved it – it was like spending a day at the fun fair!

But now I've got a different kind of expedition in mind. A dizzying journey into the very extremities of words. A journey into places both dark and bright, wild and strange. A journey where you will see and hear and read things that will make you gasp and laugh and shake your head with wonder and astonishment – and maybe with even a tiny trickle of fear . . .

If you come with me now, together we will discover old words and new words, old languages and new languages, secret languages and silent languages and even invented languages. We'll wonder, how do we speak, how do we listen, how do we write? And even more perplexing, what do we really mean?

That's enough of my crazy chatter. Are you willing? Are you ready? Come on, get on your hiking boots, find your telescope, your binoculars and your torch. Pull your backpack over your shoulders and have every single one of your wits about you.

Onwards! Avanti! Vamos!

In other words, let's go!

From your fellow adventurer,

The Word Spy

Contents

1. Meet the family

2. Surprising languages

3. Learning to speak

4. All the world's a stage

5. The play's the thing

6. Nouns are like ice cream

7. Verbs are like goldfish

8. What do words mean, anyway?

9. Words, words, words

10. Words wanted – dead or alive!

11. The magical act of writing

12. Buried treasure

Calling All Puzzle Hunters

Before we start, Spies – remember the secret message I left for you inside my first book, The Word Spy? Well, I've done it again.

To crack this code you need to find twelve different secret words. Yes – twelve!

This is how it works. At the end of every chapter, I've written a little rhyme. Read the rhyme carefully, and look at all the clues I've given. Then search back through the chapter you've just finished reading. Inside that chapter is the secret word you're looking for. (I wonder if you've been to the zoo lately . . .)

Once you've got all twelve words, write them down in a list, in the order of the chapters. Then, when you've made VERY sure nobody is looking, go to the back of the book, and await my instructions . . .

Yours sneakily,

The Word Spy

1. Meet the family

What Is a Language, Anyway?

Let's start our journey together with one simple word – language.

The world is full of languages – languages that millions of people speak and languages that hardly anyone speaks. Languages that are asleep and languages that are wide awake. Languages that are always changing and languages that are all mixed up.

What is a language? Well, if someone asked you that, you might start off by saying, um, it's a whole lot of words that people use to speak and read and write. (You're a Word Spy, after all!)

But a language is more than a whole lot

of words. Think about it. If you couldn't speak English, and found yourself in an English-speaking country, it wouldn't be enough just to get hold of an English dictionary and read the words out when you needed them.

It would help you a bit, of course. I mean, if you were about to be stung by a giant bee, you could quickly get out your English dictionary and look up the word 'bee' and scream:

'BEE! BEE!'

Hopefully everyone would know what you meant and come over and help you get away safely.

But what if you wanted to say a bit more? Like, what if you wanted directions to the nearest Bee Museum? Or where you could buy a plastic blow-up bee for your favourite auntie's birthday?

If you just stood there screaming 'Bee, bee!' you wouldn't get very far. You could try looking up 'where', 'plastic', 'inflatable' and even 'auntie', but by then everyone would be very confused and start looking around for your inflatable Auntie Bea. (Or they might just call the police.)

Language is what will help you. Language is the way human beings string meanings together in endlessly different combinations, so that we can say millions of different things for all the millions of different situations that we find ourselves in.

All through history, all over the world, there have been thousands of ways of doing this. That's what we call 'languages'. In the world at the moment there are at least 6000 different languages spoken, heard, signed, seen, read or written, and there are thousands more that were used in the past.

Family Reunion

That's a lot of languages! When you've got as many as that, and you want to think about them, you have to find a way to put them in groups, so you don't go crazy. One way is to group them into families.

They're not exactly like the families we're used to, with uncles and aunties and cousins and grannies. They don't send each other birthday cards or have meals together or go on family holidays or give each other silly nicknames.

Languages are grouped into families by people who study languages. It's a way of organising a LOT of information. Look at plants and animals. We classify them as families too. The cat family, the dog family, the turtle family, the lettuce family. (Personally I'd love to meet a family of lettuces.)

Anyway, you know how in families often people look alike or sound alike, or have the same annoying habits? I mean, imagine if one day you met a stranger who looked EXACTLY like your Uncle Ethelred and even winked in the same way every time he saw a duck walking by.

You would think, Hey, I must be related to this person somehow!

This is more or less how it works in languages too. If there are enough similarities between two languages and it looks like they can be traced back to the same ancestor, they are put into the same family.

A Piece of Pie

Now, some languages have HUGE families, with hundreds of members. Indonesian belongs to a very big family like this. Other languages, like Hungarian, have small families with just a few members. And then some languages don't seem to have ANY family members at all! The language of the Basque people in Spain is thought to be one of these lonely languages. But maybe some day someone will track down some of their relations . . .

English belongs to one of the bigger families. It's called the Indo-European family. You might be surprised to meet some of the family members, because they can seem very different. Hindi, Greek, Persian, Russian, French, Gaelic,

German, Spanish, Armenian and more – believe it or not, they are in the same family as English. Yep, they all share a great-great-great-great-great-great-great-great-great-great-great-great-great-great-great-grandparent language called Proto-Indo-European – or PIE for short.

Linguists (experts in languages) think that PIE may have been spoken as far back as 4000 BC, perhaps in Russia, perhaps in India, perhaps

in Turkey. Nobody is really sure. But wherever it began, from there it spread as people moved and settled in different places around the world. Slowly the way each group of people spoke began to change, and PIE transformed itself into hundreds of different languages.

(Hmm, what language do you speak? Oh, just a bit of Proto-Indo-European!)

Many Tongues

Have you ever met someone with more than one tongue? Eek! That sounds disgusting. But when I say 'tongue' here, I don't mean the floppy pink thing inside your mouth. I mean 'language'.

You've probably heard the expression 'mother tongue'. Your mother tongue is the language you grew up speaking, also known as your 'first language'. Some people never get past their first language – their first language ends up also being their last language. This is especially true of people whose mother tongue is English. Because English is so widespread, often its speakers don't get the chance or feel the need to learn another tongue.

But most children in the world grow up speaking two or more languages. They might live in a country where more than one language is spoken or they might migrate to a place where another language is spoken. Sometimes children will speak one language with their parents at home and another language at school or with their friends. They may even end up having conversations in more than one language at a time!

Many people also learn another language for work, business, travel – or just for fun. Someone who can speak a lot of languages is called a *polyglot*, which means 'many tongues' in Greek. And a person who knows ten, twenty or even fifty languages is called a *hyperpolyglot* – 'super-many-tongues'. A British politician called Sir John Bowring, who lived 200 years ago, was said to be able to speak 100 languages!

He was certainly hyper-something . . .

Shhhh, That Language Is Sleeping

While we're on the subject, did you know you can learn to speak a language, and then seem to completely forget it?

Look at the strange case of a ship cabin boy, Narcisse Pelletier. He was born in France, so naturally he grew up speaking French. But in 1858, at the age of 14, he was abandoned in Cape York in northern Australia, after a terrible shipwreck. So he went to live with the local Aboriginal people, and learnt to speak their language, Uutaalnganu.

When he was discovered 17 years later by an English ship and taken back to France, he had completely forgotten all his French, and could only speak Uutaalnganu. This is what happens if you don't use a language for a long time. It seems to disappear from your brain altogether.

But wait – Narcisse's French language wasn't really gone! It was actually only dormant, which means 'sleeping'. And when a language is dormant, it can be woken up. At first Narcisse didn't understand any French at all. (Please, somebody speak Uutaalnganu!) But then mysteriously, in fact within a few weeks, the French he learnt as a child started to return, no longer dormant but WIDE AWAKE.

It's Official

An official language is not the language you speak at the office. It means a language that a government recognises as important to their country, usually because a lot of people speak it.

Many countries have a single official language, but some countries have more than one. New Zealand, for example, has three official languages: English, Maori and New Zealand Sign Language. Singapore has four official languages: English, Malay, Mandarin and Tamil. And India has 22 official languages! (Good place for a polyglot.)

And then there are countries that have no official language at all. Neither Australia, the United States of America or the United Kingdom has one. Although I guess you could say English is the non-official official language.

Endangered, Dying . . .

Although there are thousands of them out there, languages, like pandas or dinosaurs, can become threatened, endangered and finally extinct. Of the 6000 or so languages in the world today, linguists think that 3000 of them could disappear in the next hundred years. Aaagh! What is killing them? Is it some strange disease? Not exactly.

Languages die in different ways. All through history, rulers have banned languages in order to make everyone speak the same language. Kings of Britain put bans on Welsh, Scottish and Irish languages, for example, because they wanted everyone to speak English. They thought that would help make everybody more obedient. Several Spanish governments have tried to ban the Catalan language of the people of north-eastern Spain for the same reason.

Elsewhere, in places such as North America, Australia and New Zealand, the languages of indigenous people have sometimes been banned in schools, and the children have been told only to speak English. This has meant some of the languages have disappeared.

One problem is, most children whose first language is spoken by just a small number of people will end up learning another language that has many more speakers, like English. After all, if you only spoke a language known by a few thousand people or a few hundred or even less, there would be lots of things you wouldn't be able to do. It would be hard to make new friends beyond those few hundred people. You could only read books or see movies that were in your language. You might not be able to study at school or go to university or get work, except with people who spoke your language.

Learning another language that many people speak means there will be more things that you will be able to do. Still, it doesn't mean you have to give up the old one! After all, most people in the world are bilingual or even multilingual.

But a huge language like English can almost suffocate the smaller languages, and make it very hard for them to survive.

Dead

Ah, the death of a language is such a sad thing. Look at all the mystery and history we Word Spies have learnt the English language contains. It's the same for any language. It grew up in its unique place and time, and has all sorts of secrets about how human beings think and feel hidden inside. When a language dies, all of that disappears as well. And if the language has not been written down anywhere, it will be gone forever.

There's a language called Batjamalh, spoken by the Wadjiginy people of the Northern Territory of Australia. A woman named Esther Burrenjuck is thought to be the last fluent speaker left . . .

Raising the Dead

When a language dies out completely, and there are no speakers left, it is classified as extinct. But there have been some startling cases of raising the dead!

Hebrew, the language in which most of the Bible was originally written, more or less died out as a spoken language by the second century AD. But then nearly two thousand years later, in the 19th century, some people decided to try to revive it.

They could do this because Hebrew was a written language as well as a spoken language and they could use the Bible as a reference book. That way they taught their children to speak Hebrew, and their friends and their friends' friends. When new people came to live near them, they spoke to them in Hebrew, too.

And it worked. Now Hebrew, along with Arabic, is an official language of Israel, spoken by millions of people.

Not Dead Yet . . .

Latin is a language
As dead as dead can be
First it killed the Romans
And now it's killing me!

British children used to chant this rhyme about being made to learn Latin at school. Latin is the language the ancient Romans used to speak.

But actually, Latin's not really dead. I wonder if you've ever heard of 'Romance languages'? These are not languages that are good to know if you are going on a romantic date!

If you look at the word 'romance', you can see 'roman' inside it. That's what a Romance language is, one that comes from the language of the ancient Romans – in other words, Latin.

The main Romance languages are French, Spanish, Portuguese, Italian and Romanian. They are all quite different, both from each other and from Latin, but that's where they started.

Time Travel

If a group of Latin-speaking Romans were to go on a time-travel tour to one of the countries where Romance languages are spoken, they wouldn't understand much of what people said. But they'd be able to pick up something from the written language, because so many of the words are based on Latin.

Imagine you're a Latin-speaking tourist from ancient Rome and you find yourself in a country in Europe or South America where a Romance language is spoken. You can't understand what anyone is saying to you, but you can sort of recognise two Latin words in a newspaper headline – *vacca*, which means 'cow', and *luna*, which means 'moon'. Here are the headlines. Can you work out what might have happened?

Italian La vacca saltò oltre la luna

Spanish La vaca saltó sobre la luna

Romanian Vaca a sarit peste lună

French La vache sautait à travers la lune

You've got it – the cow jumped over the moon!

LA VACA SALTÓ
SOBRE LA LUNA

E X C L U S I V O!

Tower of Babel

Okay, so there are thousands of languages. But why so many? Why don't we all speak the same language? Wouldn't that be a lot easier?

I guess asking why there are so many languages is a bit like asking why there are so many kinds of cucumbers. (There are thousands of types of cucumber out there!) Diversity – difference – seems to be the natural state of the world. People living in different places, doing different things under different conditions, eat differently, dress differently, and, yes, speak differently.

There are lots of myths and legends that try to explain why there are so many languages, and usually the gods had something to do with it! One of the most famous stories is from the book of Genesis in the Bible, about the Tower of Babel.

According to this story, in the beginning of the world humans all spoke the same language. Then one day, being curious, they all got together and began to build a high tower up to the sky, to see what was going on up there. God didn't think much of that, and, as a punishment, he split the one language up into many languages. The idea was to stop such a thing ever happening again. If people couldn't understand each other, how would they get together and build anything?

Ah, which leads me to . . .

Dr Hopeful

Esperanto.

I'm sure you've heard of artificial flowers, but have you ever heard of an artificial language? This is a language that someone has deliberately invented.

Wow! Imagine inventing a whole language! One of the most famous artificial languages is called Esperanto and it was invented by an eye doctor named Lazarus Ludwig Zamenhof. His pen name was Doktoro Esperanto, which means 'Dr Hopeful' in – you've guessed it – Esperanto.

Dr Hopeful, I mean, Dr Zamenhof grew up in Poland over a hundred years ago. He had a lot of languages in his head – Russian, Yiddish, Polish, Hebrew, French, German, Latin, Greek and English. What a headache! No wonder he began thinking about how much better it would be if we could all speak ONE language.

He didn't mean that people should stop speaking their own loved languages. What he wanted was an international second language that you could use to talk with anyone in the world. So he set about inventing a totally new language, which is what we now know as Esperanto.

Dr Zamenhof tried to make the rules of Esperanto as simple and sensible as possible, so that you could learn it in a matter of weeks. He based it on the languages that he already knew. Here are some words and phrases you can try out on your friends:

English	Esperanto
Hello	*Saluton*
My name is...	*Mi nomiĝas...* (pronounced nomee-jas)
What's your name?	*Kiel vi nomiĝas?* (key-el)
How are you?	*Kiel vi fartas?* (farrrr-tas)
Good	*Bone* (bon-eh)
Not good	*Ne bone*
Thank you	*Dankon*
Please	*Bonvole* (bon-vole-eh)
Where is the bathroom?	*Kie estas la necesejo?* (kee-eh estas la nets-eh-seh-yo)
I don't know	*Mi ne scias* (sts-eeas)

The quick brown fox?

You should be able to work out at least a bit of Esperanto if you see it written down. Have a go at this sentence (you might need your English dictionary):

> *La rapida bruna hundo saltis super*
> *la maldiligenta vulpo.*

HINTS:

* *La* means 'the', like in French.
* You can guess *rapida*!
* If someone is a brunette, it means their hair is which colour?
* *Hundo* – do you know another, more common word for 'hound'?
* A somersault, remember, is a kind of jump.
* If something is superior, it means it's above other things.
* 'Mal' often means 'bad' in English – like malicious or malevolent. A 'diligent' student is one that works hard. So put

these two meanings together and see if you can find a word for it.

* In English, 'vulpine' means like which crafty animal?

Esperanto parolata – Esperanto spoken here

If you want to hear what Esperanto sounds like, there are plenty of sites on the internet that have clips of people speaking it. Over a million people today speak and read Esperanto, in countries all round the world. There's poetry, there are novels, children's books and text books. And there was even a movie made entirely in

Esperanto! It's a science-fiction story called *Incubus*, starring the *Star Trek* actor William Shatner.

Poor Dr Zamenhof hoped that if everyone could understand each other, wars would not happen so easily. He died, still hopeful, in 1917, in the middle of World War One. And sadly his three children were killed by the Nazis in World War Two. Adolf Hitler, the leader of the Nazis in Germany, didn't like Esperanto at all. He wasn't the only one – governments all over the world have been suspicious of Esperanto. Who knows what people might get up to if we all spoke one language?

Crocodiling

By the way, there's a great expression in Esperanto, *Ne krokodilu!* This translates as 'Don't crocodile!'. What on earth does this mean?

Well, 'crocodiling' in Esperanto is when two people who have both learnt to speak Esperanto start speaking to each other in another language. Tsk, tsk. Stop that crocodiling right now! (And stop alligatoring too while you're at it.)

Speaking Frankly

The wish for a common language between different groups of people is much older than Esperanto. You might know the phrase 'lingua franca'. *Lingua* means 'language' in Italian, and *franca* means 'of the Franks'. The Franks were a tribe who had an empire in Europe over a thousand years ago. In the Middle Ages, when European people travelled and traded with people from Middle Eastern and African countries, they communicated with a mixture of their languages. This new mixed-up way of speaking was called 'lingua franca' – the European language.

Nowadays, lingua franca means any language that's used as a common language. It doesn't have to be a mixed up-language – in fact, English is the world's most popular lingua franca, as it's the most common second language that people learn. It's estimated that about a third of the people in the world understand at least some English.

Pidgin

Pidgin is another kind of common language – and it's got nothing to do with birds!

A hundred years ago or so, when people from China and Britain were trading they found it too hard to learn each other's language, so they started speaking a mixture of English and Chinese for business. They called this mixed-up language *Pidgin*, which is thought to be the Chinese version of the English word 'business'.

Because the British roamed all over the world, trading, working and setting up colonies, there are many pidgins based on English, from

Japan to Nigeria to Pitcairn Island. But pidgins can be based on any language. There are pidgins of Arabic, French, Spanish, Dutch, German and many many more. In the 18th century there was even a Chinese-Russian pidgin! Apparently some of the Russians who learnt this language actually thought they were speaking Chinese . . .

Tok Pisin

Sometimes when a pidgin is spoken over many years and it becomes the first language people learn to speak, it's no longer called a pidgin, but turns into a unique language all of its own.

This is what happened to a pidgin that began in Papua New Guinea, now known as the language Tok Pisin.

Papua New Guinea is a group of islands in the South Pacific Ocean, to the north of Australia. About six million people live there, and they speak – wait for it – over EIGHT HUNDRED languages! Some of the languages have thousands of speakers, others only hundreds. There is nowhere in the world like it.

With so many languages, they really needed a common language for everyone to be able to speak to each other. A pidgin began when English and German traders arrived about 200 years ago. It was English mixed up with German, Malay, Spanish, Portuguese and Pacific languages, and a few other bits and pieces as well. At first this pidgin was used mainly for work, but over time people began speaking it at home, too. Now it is the main official language of Papua New Guinea, and newspapers, books, television and radio are all in Tok Pisin.

Even though it started off with English, English-speakers can't understand Tok Pisin without learning it as a separate language.

Try for yourself. Have a look at the first few lines of this folk tale. Can you work out what it means? You might be able to spot a word that looks like an English word, for example, 'good' or 'sleep' or 'true'. Which word do you think means 'kangaroo'?

Tok Pisin

Bipo bipo tru, Dok na Sikau tupela i save poroman gut tru. Tupela i save slip wantaim, painim abus wantaim na pilai wantaim. Tupela i kamap nambawan poroman tru.

English

Long, long ago, Dog and Kangaroo were very good friends. They often slept together, hunted wild game together, and played together. They became the best of friends.

An anagram
May give a clue
To find the word
That baffles you

ELUTRT

Hmm, does anyone remember what an anagram is? You might have to look in my first book, The Word Spy, to find out!

2.

Surprising languages

The Sounds of Silence

Usually when you think of language, you think of people speaking. But remember there are also silent languages.

Silent languages have existed for as long as people have been unable to hear or speak. They are often called 'sign languages' because people who use them make signs with their hands, face and body. You may use sign language yourself, or know someone who does. Or you may have been to a play or heard someone give a speech where another person stands at the front translating the spoken words into sign language. It's spell-binding to watch as the language flows through the person's face and their whole body.

But it's not just a matter of waving your hands about in the air. Sign languages are as complex as spoken languages. And just as people speak different languages in different countries, so there are thousands of different sign languages all over the world, with different words and ways of making sentences. This means that when people who use sign language in different countries can't communicate with each other, you get pidgin or mixed-up sign languages, too. And there's even an international sign language, which is used at big events like sports tournaments.

Most people who use sign language grow up bilingual. This means that as well as sign language, they learn the spoken languages of the country they are born in. So in Australia, deaf children learn Auslan, the Australian sign language, but they also usually learn English. They learn to read and write in English.

It's a bit of a one-way street though. While deaf people can usually understand the world of speaking people, it doesn't often work the other way round. Not too many hearing people learn sign language.

The Quiet Island

But it doesn't have to be like that. On the island of Martha's Vineyard in the United States over a hundred years ago, sign language was used and understood by both deaf and hearing people in entire villages. How did that happen?

Well, you see, there were many more deaf people born on Martha's Vineyard at that time than in most places. It was common for deaf people to marry people who weren't deaf, and then they had children who may or may not have been deaf. Many families on the island had at least one deaf member. After a while, this meant that pretty much everybody on the island knew somebody who couldn't hear.

As a result, sign language was everywhere. It was used in shops, in church, in school, on the street – wherever people met. Here's a memory of one of the islanders, about what life was like back then, waiting for the post at the general store:

'We would sit around and wait for the mail to come in and just talk. And the deaf would be there, everyone would be there . . . and oftentimes people would tell stories and make signs at the same time so everyone could follow him together. Of course, sometimes if there were more deaf than hearing people there, everyone would speak sign language.'

The children of Martha's Vineyard grew up bilingual, knowing both English and sign language. Imagine how handy it would have been to be able to chat with your friends in silent sign language during a boring lesson! You'd have to make sure the teacher couldn't see you though, because of course the teachers all knew sign language, too.

Living on an island cut off from the mainland of America, the people of Martha's Vineyard could run their society how they liked, and that was how they liked it, with both languages. But it didn't last long. By the 20th century, travel became easier and deaf children were sent to the mainland to be educated in bigger schools with more resources.

That was a good thing in many ways, but it meant that gradually fewer and fewer deaf people lived on the island, and hearing people stopped learning to sign. The quiet world of Martha's Vineyard became just like everywhere else. So something was lost as well.

How Do You Spell That?

Because sign language is as complex as spoken language, it takes quite a while to learn if you haven't grown up with it.

When The Word Spy was at school there was a class of children who were deaf and they had teachers who used sign language. But so that we could all communicate with each other, even a little bit, we were all taught finger spelling.

Finger spelling is using your fingers to make special signs that show each different letter of the alphabet. People who use sign languages often use a bit of finger spelling at the same time as sign language to spell out particular words – place names and things like that.

It's a pretty slow way to communicate – imagine if you spoke to someone spelling every word out separately! (T-h-a-t w-o-u-l-d t-a-k-e a-g-e-s.) Even the quickest dactylologist (a fancy word for finger speller) can only spell about 50 or 60 English words a minute. That might sound like quite a lot, but normal speech is usually at least 150 words a minute.

And of course, the problem with finger spelling is you have to be able to spell! On the opposite page is a finger-spelling alphabet. It looks complicated, but it's not too hard. Why not first try to spell your name, and then your friend's name? You'll soon get the hang of it. And then you could hold a Finger Spelling Bee!

D-o-l-l

Helen Keller was an American writer who became both deaf and blind after a bad illness as a small child. She learnt to communicate with her teacher, Miss Sullivan, by touch and by finger spelling. On the next page, read her description of the great excitement when, at the age of seven, her world slowly and magically began to open up.

The morning after my teacher came she led me into her room and gave me a doll . . . When I had played with it a little while, Miss Sullivan slowly spelled into my hand the word 'd-o-l-l'. I was at once interested in this finger play and tried to imitate it.

Running downstairs to my mother I held up my hand and made the letters for doll . . .

In the days that followed I learnt to spell a great many words, among them pin, hat, cup and a few verbs like sit, stand and walk. But my teacher had been with me several weeks before I understood that everything has a name.

Reading in the Dark

Helen Keller, although she was blind, loved reading. But how did she read if she couldn't see the words on the page? Well, it was because of an amazing writing system known as braille.

If you've ever had the chance to pass your fingers over the top of a page of braille, you'll know it's a fascinating experience. To think all those little raised dots on the page represent wonderful, surprising words, just as the letters of the alphabet do on this page. If you see someone reading braille, their fingers move so quickly and you can see their face change as the words slip silently into their mind.

Braille was devised by a man named Louis Braille over 150 years ago in France. He lost his sight as a little boy when a tool fell into his eye. He was sent to a special school for blind children. He was a very clever student who loved reading. In his school were some specially made books, which he could read by feeling the shapes of letters on the page. But there weren't very many of them, because they were very expensive to produce.

Louis Braille was obviously one of those people who are always saying to themselves, 'How can I make things better?' When he was fifteen, he learnt about a code made up of dots on paper that you could feel with your fingers. This code, called 'night writing', was used by French soldiers to pass each other messages to read in the dark. Louis thought he could use this method to create books for people who were blind, like him.

Inspired by night writing, he eventually invented his own system. This is what is now known as braille. Each letter of the alphabet is represented by six dots, raised or flat, each differently arranged in a rectangle. There are dots for the punctuation marks as well.

Arrgh! That sounds impossible! How can people read that with their fingers? Actually, it's much harder to learn to read braille if you're not blind. People who can see the dots find they have to wear an eye mask to learn it, so they're not distracted and can concentrate on the feelings in their fingertips.

There are many reading systems for people who cannot see to read, and these days there are also brilliant computer programs that read texts and then speak them out loud. But the most famous and beautiful method of all is still braille.

This is what the braille alphabet looks like:

A B C D E F G

H I J K L M N

O P Q R S T U

V W X Y Z

Capital Letter Full Stop

Scissors Paper Rock

I bet you've played the game Scissors Paper Rock. It's a very old game all based on gestures. Versions of it are played all over the world, with names like *schnick, schnack, schnuck* (in Germany), *jan-ken-pon* (in Japan) or *kai-bai-bo* (in Korea).

Gestures in games like this seem to be the same everywhere. But sometimes a gesture can mean different things in a different culture. A simple nod of the head to most people means 'yes'. But in parts of Bulgaria and Greece, a kind of nod can actually mean 'no'. (Yes, I mean, no.)

Even in the same culture, gestures can have double meanings. Think of 'fingers crossed'.

It can either mean you're wishing someone good luck, or that what you're saying is a lie.

And sometimes what you think you're saying with a gesture may not be that clear at all. When The Word Spy was standing in an ice-cream shop recently, her mobile phone rang. As she went outside to take the call, she turned to the woman serving and held up two fingers, meaning 'I'll just be two minutes'. Only, the woman thought she meant 'two ice creams please', and had them ready and waiting on The Word Spy's return.

Oh well, lucky they were delicious!

The Language of the Road

You can make gestures with your hands, your face, your whole body. But did you know you can also make gestures in writing? Just think of the range of symbols used in the beautiful, mysterious 'dot' paintings of the Aboriginal people in Australia. Some of the symbols are thousands of years old and are used to express ideas, thoughts, stories and feelings. You can see some on the next page.

Aboriginal Symbols

Rainbow or cloud or cliff or sandhill

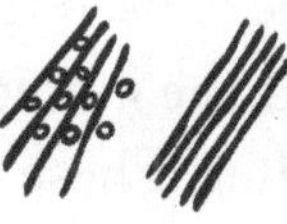
Rain

Man

Two men sitting

Fire or smoke or water or blood

Usually means four women sitting

Camp site, stone, well, rock hole, breast, fire hole or fruit

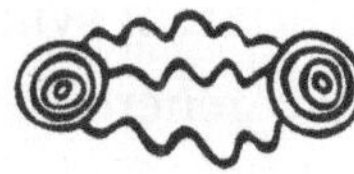
Waterholes connected by running water

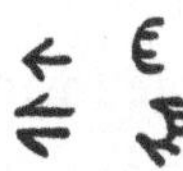
Footprints

Sitting-down place

Clouds, boomerangs or windbreaks

Star

Can mean water, rainbow, snake, lightning, string, cliff or honey store

Travelling sign with circles as resting place

Another intriguing although very different set of written gestures is known as 'the language of the road', which has been used for centuries by people who wandered the country on foot looking for work and shelter. These travelling workers, even if they didn't know each other, wanted to let the others like them know if a farm or house was a good or a bad place to approach. So they started leaving each other secret messages – symbols scratched on a wall or fence or tree trunk, with chalk or a pencil or a knife, whatever they had.

There were different symbols to show if the people inside were generous and would give you work and a good dinner; or that you shouldn't knock on this door, because the people were really mean and nasty and might set vicious dogs on you. There were symbols to show if the drinking water was bad, or if there was a nice haystack to sleep in. There were even symbols to say that you'd better tell these people a really sad story if you wanted any help!

Nowadays people travelling and working on the road are more likely to use mobile phones to swap this sort of information, so the old 'language of the road' has probably died away.

Although there's always graffiti tags, of course . . . but that's another story altogether!

Here are some examples of traditional 'hobo' or 'swaggie' symbols. Why not use them to write some messages of your own?

Click Click

Okay, so that's communicating without making much noise. What about some louder ways of getting the message across?

In English, we sometimes make a clicking noise with our tongue when we feel sorry for someone or disapprove of something. (Tsk tsk!) But did you know that in some African languages, clicks like these are used in ordinary words? Different clicks are used for different sounds inside words.

The most famous of the clicking languages is from South Africa. It's called Xhosa. Try pronouncing it with a clicking sound in your throat – 'K(click)osa'. Xhosa actually has fifteen separate clicks! They are made by using various parts of the mouth, tongue, throat and nose.

It's probably hard to understand without hearing it. The South African singer Miriam Makeba sang a Xhosa wedding song, known in English as 'The Knock Knock Beetle' or 'The Click Song'. See if you can find a recording of it.

Whistle While You Work

Although it sounds like something in a story, there really are places in the world where people communicate by whistling. In parts of China, Greece, Turkey, Spain and Mexico, you might hear people working in the fields whistling to each other. The sound of a whistle carries further than a voice, which means you don't have to shout if you want to talk to someone far away. Whistled messages are usually pretty simple, like 'I think it's going to rain', or 'Have you seen my hat?'.

On the Canary Islands in the Atlantic Ocean, there's a kind of whistling used by shepherds, known as *El Silbo*, from the Spanish word *silbato*, which means 'whistle'. Talking in whistles has been passed on from parent to child for hundreds of years, and now it's even taught in school. Look it up on the internet and have a listen for yourself. It's amazing – it sounds like mysterious bird calls . . .

(Just so you know, the name 'Canary Islands' has nothing to do with the fact that canaries whistle! It comes from the Latin word for dog, *canis*, because the islands were once famous for their fierce dogs.)

Twin Language

If you are a twin, or you know some twins, then you might have heard about how some very young twins speak to each other in what seems like a foreign language. They understand each other all right, but nobody else can. They use their own words for things and have their own way of making sentences. Sometimes this is called twin language.

Twins, of course, grow up with someone exactly their size and age to talk to. That's quite different from just having your parents or big brothers and sisters. It's natural that while they are so small and learning language they develop their own unique ways of saying things to each other.

Twins who do this usually stop after a year or two, and by the time they go to school they speak like everyone else. But a famous pair of identical twins in the United States, Grace and Virginia Kennedy, were still speaking their secret language at eight years old!

The Kennedy twins were unusual, as they lived quite lonely lives away from other children. They were looked after a lot by their German-speaking grandmother while their parents were at work, so they developed a strange mixture of English and German. But they also had special words they seemed to make up for reasons of their own.

For example, for a pencil they said *pinto*, and *nieps* for a knife, and *toolaymeia* for spaghetti. They had 30 different ways to say the word potato! (They must have really loved potatoes . . .) A film was made about them called *Poto and Cabengo*. This was their way of saying their own names, Grace and Virginia.

It's not only twins who make up secret languages. Sometimes friends do it, too. In a book called *The Secret Language*, by Ursula Nordstrom, two girls at an American boarding school make up a language that only they can understand. It helps them feel less lonely and makes their friendship very special.

Have you ever made up your own secret language?

If I Could Talk with the Animals

If you have a pet, you'll know the feeling you get when you look into its eyes and it looks so intently back at you, as though it's trying to tell you something. If only your dog or cat or budgie or even your guinea pig could talk, how wonderful it would be! (Actually, I don't know if my guinea pig would be *that* interesting . . .)

Have you heard of Doctor Dolittle?

'Now listen, Doctor, and I'll tell you something. Did you know that animals can talk?'

'I knew that parrots can talk,' said the Doctor.

'Oh, we parrots can talk in two languages – people's language and bird-language,' said Polynesia proudly. 'If I say, "Polly wants a cracker," you understand me. But hear this: Ka-ka oi-ee, fee-fee?'

'Good Gracious!' cried the Doctor. 'What does that mean?'

'That means, "Is the porridge hot yet?" – in bird-language.'

'My! You don't say so!' said the Doctor. 'You never talked that way to me before.'

'What would have been the good?' said Polynesia, dusting some cracker-crumbs off her left wing. 'You wouldn't have understood me if I had.'

Doctor Dolittle was the man who could talk with the animals. You may have read the books about him by the British writer Hugh Lofting, or seen one of the movies with Eddie Murphy playing the doctor.

Animals obviously communicate, both with each other and with us, in complex and fascinating ways. Look at whale songs – they seem to us to be full of mysterious meanings. See if you can find some recordings on the internet, you'll be entranced. But we can't really understand what they mean.

People have tried to teach animals our language. There are parrots that have learnt to speak over a hundred different words, and gorillas and chimpanzees who have been taught to recognise and produce words in sign language.

But even these clever animals don't seem able to use those words to create the kinds of complex sentences that a five-year-old human can. If there is a way we could communicate with animals through language, we're still a long, long way off discovering it.

My favourite talking animal

One place you will always find talking animals, though, is in stories. Books, movies and cartoons are full of talking animals.

Some people hate the thought of talking animals, and think it's silly or disrespectful. But many readers and writers love them, and there have been some wonderful books written about talking animals.

Talking animals go right back to the very beginnings of storytelling, and are found in some of the most ancient myths in cultures all over the world. The stories of the Australian Aboriginal Dreamtime are full of talking animals. In the Bible there's a talking snake, and even a talking donkey! And I'm sure you've heard of Aesop's Fables, very short stories that were written in Greece in the 6th century BC, about talking foxes, bears, bees, geese, horses, hares, grasshoppers, you name it.

The Word Spy's favourite talking animal is the Muddle-headed Wombat from the books by Ruth Park. If you haven't met Wombat and his friends Mouse and Tabby, on the opposite page is a little snippet of his adventures to read for yourself. Wombat has a very particular way of talking!

If you were writing a story about a talking animal, which animal would you choose? (I'd like a talking tortoise, myself . . .)

From The Muddle-headed Wombat

'Oh Wombat,' cried Mouse anxiously, forgetting how cross it was. 'Did that horrid dog bite you?'

'No,' said Wombat. Then he confessed. 'Promise you'll never tell my terribubble secret, Mouse. Promise, Tab? Aw right then. That dog sat on me, just imaginabubble!'

Tabby thought it was very fair.

'Just think of the people you've sat on,' he pointed out.

'Yes, but that's for wombats to do,' said Wombat.

Inside these lines
The word you'll see
If you read them
*Carefully**

Hopping Outrageously Ruins
Scrambled Eggs

*Is it an acronym – or a backronym?
Ah, better consult The Word Spy.

3.

Learning to speak

First Words

Word Spies, do you know what your first word was? Ask your parents – they should remember.

The first word most parents hear their babies say is 'mummy' or 'mama'. (Aaahh . . .) But it can be 'daddy' or any other name or word that is important to them. I know a child whose first word was 'teddy'. And you know Lisa Simpson on *The Simpsons*? Her first word was 'Bart'!

Most babies are about a year old when they say their very first word. But that doesn't mean you were quiet for those first twelve months. You would have made a lot of noise. Not words exactly, but something called 'babble'.

I'm sure you've heard a baby babbling. They sit in their strollers or lie on the floor staring up at the ceiling and open their mouths and off they go – 'bababababababa, dadadadad, oooooo-mooogoodooooo'. Babies love to babble (when they're not crying, that is). 'Gaggaaaabooo-babababababababa' – it can seem like they really mean something!

If you've read Lemony Snicket's *A Series of Unfortunate Events* you will know that baby Sunny is always coming out with strange sounds. Luckily the author seems to know what she means:

> *'Wonic,' Sunny said, which probably meant, 'And learning secretarial skills is an exciting opportunity for me, although I should really be in nursery school instead.'*

Dog, Dogs, Dogs!!!!!

When you were a baby, you would have babbled away for about a year. All the time you would have been listening hard as well, and learning to understand lots of words, even if you couldn't say them. Then finally you would have opened your mouth and spoken that long-awaited word that other people could understand. Hurray!

Then you would have said another word. And another, and another, and another.

On they tumbled. In fact, in the next six months or so, you would have learnt to say around fifty words – and understood many, many more.

Okay, so you learnt all those words. But just knowing words alone is not enough, remember. You need to learn how to use those words in different ways, depending on what you want to say at the time.

Let's say one of the first words you learnt when you were little was 'dog'. You probably said it in a nice big loud voice – 'DOG'. But what if you wanted to say you liked the dog? 'DOG' isn't enough. You'd have to say something like 'NICE DOG'. Or that you were scared of the dog? 'BAD DOG.' Or what if a hundred dogs were running down the street towards you? You'd want to say, 'DOGS! DOGS! DOGS!'

This is making language. Slowly, slowly, bit by bit every day, little humans learn how to change words and add words together to make different meanings. There's a lot to learn. Believe it or not, by the time you were five, you had learnt SO much, you could speak more or less like an adult.

That Child Is a Genius

If you find that hard to believe, read this:

> 'Give me back my teddy bear right now! And all my little blue bunnies. If you don't, I'm telling my mummy and she's going to be very angry and you're going to be in BIG trouble, you are, so there!'

That's the sort of thing you might hear your little brother or sister say. And there are a lot of pretty complicated things going on there. If you were learning another language, it would take you a long time to learn to say all that.

In a grammar book (the sort of book that tries to explain how language works), it might tell you that this little speech contains things like verbs, nouns, adjectives, conjunctions and personal pronouns, and the imperative and subjunctive moods, the future and past tense – STOP! STOP! Wow! You didn't know your little sister was such a genius, did you?

Brilliant Mistakes

But wait a minute, you say. Little kids are not so smart. They're always making mistakes.

I guess if you have a little brother or sister who is just learning to speak, you probably think there's not much you can learn from them, especially from their mistakes. But you're wrong!

I'll show you what I mean. When The Word Spy's nephew Tarquino was three, his father handed him a lovely plate of peas for dinner. He took one look at it and burst into tears, saying:

'I don't like these little green eggs!'

We think this is funny because we know that eggs are much bigger than peas and that they are definitely not green. (Okay, maybe in Dr Seuss.) We also know that eggs are things that are laid by chickens (oh all right, and crocodiles), whereas peas are vegetables that grow in the ground.

We know all these things because we have been in the world longer than three years. But Tarquino couldn't help not knowing all that. He was trying to understand the world through the things he *did* know.

He knew that an 'egg' was something roundish that his father put on his plate for him to eat. So when he saw something with a similar shape being offered as food, he thought it must also be an 'egg'. The shape of something was more important at that point in his life than the size or the colour.

This is a very normal way of learning. It even has a special name: over-extension. Over-extension is what happens when you learn the word for one thing, and then you over-extend it to something else that you think is similar.

Now imagine a little girl who has a pet rabbit. It's furry and brown and hops around the garden. When she sees a kangaroo bounding past on a country drive, she might point and say 'Bunny!'. Or if she's very clever she might say 'BIG bunny!'.

Er, I think that might be a case of over-over-extension!

The Child's Eye

It's not only little kids who do this. Writers do something very similar when they use **metaphors** and **similes** to show what two different things have in common in a way that most of us haven't noticed before.

In a simile, you'll see the word 'like' or 'as'. Here's one:

> I lay down in my sleeping bag,
> *like a sausage wrapped up in pastry.*

With a metaphor, something is written or spoken about as if it actually *is* something else, not just similar. Like this:

> I lay down in my sleeping bag. *I was a sausage, wrapped up in a pastry blanket.*

(Where's the tomato sauce?)

Stories, poems and songs are all places where you might find especially wonderful similes and metaphors. One of The Word Spy's favourite similes comes from the Bible, in the Song of Solomon:

Your hair is like a flock of goats,
moving down the slopes of Gilead.

I would like to have seen that head of hair!

If you listen carefully to what little children say, you will notice their language is full of poetry, with strange and unexpected similes and metaphors, just like those little green eggs. This is because everything is so new to them and they see connections in places we would never think of, or have forgotten.

Some of the world's most famous painters, like Matisse and Picasso, believed that if you could only look at the world through the eyes of a very small child you would find the most beautiful and extraordinary things . . .

Baby School?

So, anyway, how does it happen? How do we learn to use language when we're little to turn words into so many different thoughts and feelings and ideas?

After all, when you're grown up and you want to learn a language, you need a textbook and a teacher. You can't just run around the playground babbling away and hope to pick it up. But nobody sits a bunch of babies down in a classroom and says:

> 'He-hem, children, pay attention.
> This is how you make a sentence.
> You put the adjective here, and the verb here, and the adverb here. And you –
> STOP SUCKING YOUR THUMB!'

It wouldn't work, would it?

Across the Universe

Nobody really knows exactly how we pick up language, but there have been plenty of theories! One of the most famous ones was thought up by an American linguist called Noam Chomsky. He wondered a lot about how children learn the rules and patterns of language. He was especially interested in the mistakes children make, and how they learn to correct themselves.

He knew that often adults (or big brothers and sisters!) point out mistakes and tell children what they should say. But Chomsky still thought this doesn't happen often enough to explain how young humans learn the patterns of language so quickly. He reckoned they should make lots more mistakes than they do.

He wondered and wondered. Could there be something inside children's brains that makes them see patterns and rules in language? A kind of language-making instinct that humans are born with, a bit like the way a baby bird learns how to sing without going to school?

He decided that there was, and he gave this idea a rather strange name. He called it 'Universal Grammar'. 'Universal' because he thought every child born had it, and 'grammar' being the word he used to mean the rules and patterns of language.

Hmm, it's certainly an interesting idea. Do you think he's right?

If the word
You cannot guess
This rebus here*
Should make it less
(difficult)

**Wondering what a rebus is?*
All is revealed in The Word Spy . . .

4. All the world's a stage

Grammar

Universal or not, grammar is a word you will have come across from time to time. But what does it mean? It's a little word, only seven letters, but it's sure got a lot of ideas inside it! Sometimes it seems like a magic toy box – each time you reach into it, you pull out something completely different.

Grammar is the word we use for how people over thousands of years have thought and wondered about the way language works. Think of yourself as an explorer, going deep into an underground cave. Trying to understand grammar is like shining a torch on the walls and the roof, lighting up all the wonderful colours and rocks and stalagmites and stalactites and underground streams and waterfalls and deep pools – and oops! Be careful you don't slip and fall!

If you look on the internet or in books or ask people about grammar, you will get many different answers. But you will start to notice some words are repeated over and over again – words to do with grammar. And you might think, hmm, maybe I could understand all this stuff better if I actually knew what some of these words meant!

So that's what we're going to look at here. We're going to shine the light around, above and beneath, and see what colours and shapes we can glimpse in the darkness . . .

Curtain Up!

If you've ever been in a play, you'll know that everybody acts together on stage, but that each actor has a different part.

Well, one way to look at language is to think of a sentence as a play, and of the words as actors, each with their own role. In traditional grammar books these roles are called 'parts of speech'.

But they're a pretty unruly bunch, this troupe of actors. They march up and down on stage, together or alone. Sometimes they shout, sometimes they whisper, sometimes they all talk at once. Sometimes one actor will play more than one part, and sometimes they'll even push another actor over and take that part instead of their own!

Anyway, let's raise the curtain now and have a look for ourselves . . .

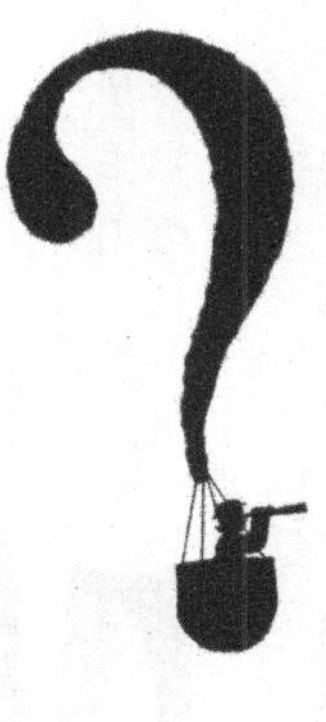

BUT
THE
TALL
DOG
WALKE
CON-
JUNCT-
ION
ARTICLE
AD-
JECT-
IVE
NOUN
VERB

QUICKLY
AFTER
ME!
GOSH!
AD-
VERB
PRE-
POS-
ITION
PRO-
NOUN
INTER-
JECT-
ION

Nouns

A noun is a name for something. Nouns are EVERYWHERE. If you look around a room, you will see that it is full of nouns.

There may be a **chair**, or a **mirror**, or a **light**. There may be a **table** with a **plate** of sliced **watermelon** on it, waiting for you to eat it up. (Let's hope so!) These things are all nouns.

Nouns can also be animals or people. If **The Word Spy** saw a **rabbit** hopping onto the **back** of a **camel** while the **cat** was talking to the **Prime Minister**, these are all nouns. (And a very unusual **situation**.)

Nouns can be places. **Rotorua** is a noun and so is the **Zambezi River** – um, actually that's two nouns. These are real places, but nouns can also be imaginary places, like **Narnia** or **Hogwarts**.

Nouns are also things we can't see or touch. Feelings, for example. If you feel **happiness**, you are feeling a noun! Or ideas – when you are learning **geography** you are learning a noun. Or actions – if you hate **snorkelling**, you're hating a noun.

The **world** sure is chockablock full of **nouns**.

Adjectives

A noun all by itself is a lonely thing. It doesn't really tell us much. To really enjoy the noun, you have to pull a few other players in.

Adjectives are generally found near nouns. The word 'adjective' comes from a Latin word which means 'to have been thrown at'. So an adjective is something you throw at a noun. (Quick, noun, duck!) It's great throwing adjectives at nouns. They make your nouns so much more interesting. For example, if I said:

'The girl has hair,'

you might think, Oh. But if I threw an adjective at it and I said:

'The girl has **green** hair,'

you might think, OH.

You can throw more than one adjective at a noun – as many as you like! They can be pretty useful. Like when my Uncle Orkall asked me:

'Would you like some **slippery** noodles?'

I was just about to say 'yes', when he helpfully threw in a few more adjectives:

'Would you like some **slippery, disgusting, rotten old slimy** noodles?'

Um, actually, no thanks, Uncle Orkall.

Articles

Articles are the words **the, a** and **an**. They always go with a noun. *Articulus* in Latin means 'little joint'. So articles are like little bony joints of the noun. They may not seem very interesting, but actually they can make quite a difference.

The is called the 'definite article'. This is because you use it when you're talking about something definite.

So when you say:

> 'I saw **the** teacher run out the door screaming,'

you show that you mean one particular teacher, not just any old teacher.

A is called the 'indefinite article' because – you've guessed it – it's not so definite. So when you say:

> 'I saw **a** teacher run out the door screaming,'

you show that you don't know which teacher it was – it could be any of them. (Hope it's not yours . . .)

An is used instead of **a** before a word that starts with a vowel (a, e, i, o, u) or a silent 'h'. Like:

> 'Only **an** aardvark would take **an** hour to have a shower.'

The is actually the most common word in the whole English language. (Give that word a lollipop – well done!)

Verbs

So, what else do you need to get meaning on the stage? Well, you could definitely use a verb.

Verbs are sometimes called 'doing words' because they're hard at work doing something. Look what the verbs **eat**, **jump** and **paddle** are doing here to help a ferret (a noun) have a much more exciting life:

> The ferret **ate** a peanut, **jumped** into a canoe and **paddled** with his tail all the way to Brazil.

That's what I call action!

Verbs are sometimes 'being words' as well, like **grow** or **become**:

> My best friend **is** a gorilla and he **grows** bigger every year.

Or 'thinking words' – words to do with what goes on inside your brain, like **wish** and **hope**:

> My mum **believes** in Santa Claus. (Aw . . .)

I **wonder** if you can **think** of some more thinking words?

Adverbs

Remember how you could throw adjectives at a noun? An adverb is a word you can throw at a verb.

Adverbs can tell you how the verb is happening. Are you tickling your big sister **slowly** or **quickly**? Is she laughing **joyfully** or **angrily**? And are you running away **fearfully** as she chases you **furiously**? You can **usually** spot this sort of adverb because it is an adjective that has **ly** on the end of it. Like **sad** plus **ly** equals **sadly**. Instant adverb!

But not every adverb ends in **ly**. Adverbs can also tell you when something happens – words like **never**, **sometimes** and **always** are also adverbs. In fact, one of the most common adverbs that you know **well** doesn't end in **ly** either. (Guessed it? **Well** done!)

Conjunctions

You know when you go to the junction of two streets? The junction is where they join together. In a way that's what conjunctions are – they're the words that join two ideas. The most common ones are **and**, **or**, and **but**.

> 'Would you like baked mouse **and** tomato sauce, **or** a nice worm salad?'

Hmm, I would really love both, **but** I'm just not hungry.

Conjunctions are very handy – they help people understand what we mean by connecting our thoughts. So instead of saying:

> 'I cannot come to your party. My guinea pig is stuck up a very tall tree.'

With a conjunction you can say:

> 'I cannot come to your party **because** my guinea pig is stuck up a very tall tree.'

(Quick! Someone call the fire brigade and help that guinea pig down!)

Interjections

You can throw an adjective at a noun, and an adverb at a verb, and you can throw an interjection anywhere you like. Like – hey! – stop interrupting.

Lots of interjections show excitement and emotion. It can be happiness:

Gosh! Wow! Boy oh boy!

Or sadness:

Oh! Alas! Woe!

Or just plain annoyance:

Tsk tsk! Ouch!

These sorts of interjections are often followed by an exclamation mark, to remind you of the excitement of the feeling. Not every interjection is exciting, though. Let me think, **um**, I know there are some that, **er**, you throw in when you can't think of something, **uh-huh**. These ones don't usually have an exclamation mark. I mean, you're not likely to say **um!** (Um, are you?)

Some interjections have been around for hundreds of years, and some are brand new. I bet you know this interjection, which has just found its way into the dictionary via *The Simpsons* – **meh**. (**D'oh!**)

Prepositions

Prepositions are useful, too. They can tell you where something is.

The catfish is **in** the bath.

Or:

The professor hid the butterfly **under** his hat.

(Ah, so that's where it went.)

Prepositions can also tell you when or how something is, as well:

In the morning the catfish was **in** a good mood (**in** the bath).

AFTER

PRE-
POS-
ITION

English has LOTS of prepositions – over a hundred. Some are very short, like **on**, **at**, **by**, **in**, **to**, **of**, **out**, **for**. Some are middle-sized, like **with, from, above, over**; and some are long, like **underneath, alongside, between, opposite**. I'm sure you can think of lots more.

Often you might use only one preposition in a sentence, but you may need more – two, three, even four. Have a look at this little dialogue between a sick child and her nurse from a famous grammar book called *Fowler's Modern English Usage*. How many prepositions are there?

Sick child: I want to be read **to**.

Nurse: What book do you want to be read **to out of**?

Sick child: Robinson Crusoe.

(Nurse goes **out** *and returns* **with** The Swiss Family Robinson.*)*

Sick child: What did you bring me that book to be read **to out of for**?

Pronouns

There are lots more parts of speech I could talk about, but I'll finish off for now with pronouns. (Phew!)

You can probably guess from how it sounds that a pronoun is a type of noun. Pronouns are words like **I, me, you, she, he, it, her, him, we, us, they, them**. 'Pro' means 'to stand in for'. So a pronoun stands in the place where you'd usually find a noun.

Using pronouns instead of repeating nouns makes it easier for other people to listen to what you're saying or to read what you've written. (That's what you call good communication!) For example, you might write this sentence in a story:

The flamingo cried because **the flamingo** was lonely.

Well, we know it's the flamingo who's lonely, so really, there's no need to say it again.

Just use a pronoun:

The flamingo cried because **he** was lonely.

That sounds better. Now, will somebody go and make friends with that poor lonely flamingo?

If with words
Your eyes are sore
*Some rhyming slang**
May please you more

My best friend has got a new fluffy **bad habit** *in a cage in the back yard.*

** If you don't know what rhyming slang is, you might need to have a look at* The Apple Pie *– oops, I mean* The Word Spy *– to find out!*

5. The play's the thing

I Hereby Sentence You

So now we've had a good look at some of the players that will make their way into your sentences. But you don't want them just running crazily all over the stage so that nobody understands what's going on. You have to get them to do what YOU want them to do. It's what they actually do that's the most important thing.

Let's start with that word, **sentence**. In court, the sentence is how many years you have to go to prison. But what is a sentence in a language? You might say, 'That's easy! When you write it down it starts with a capital letter and ends with a full stop.'

Well, sort of. But that's not the whole story.

One way of looking at a sentence is to say it needs to have a 'subject' and a 'finite verb'.

What's Your Best Subject?

Let's start with the subject. A subject can be something you study at school, like maths or history or tadpole-pond-building. Or it can be a topic of conversation, like 'My favourite cupcake' or 'Do you prefer Nintendo or PlayStation?'.

In a sentence, the subject is who or what the sentence is about. It's usually some sort of noun. And your sentence really needs a subject! Look what happens to a sentence if there's no subject:

Baked a mulberry pie.

I know what you're saying. 'He-hem, excuse me. *Who* exactly baked the mulberry pie?' Aha! That's exactly what you don't know if you don't have a subject in your sentence. So let's put one in:

The polar bear baked a mulberry pie.

That's a relief! I thought it might have been my grandmother, and what a mess she would have made . . .

The Little Things That Make Me Complete . . .

Right. So that's the subject, the polar bear. But what about that other thing, the finite verb? Erk, sounds infinitely unpleasant . . .

You know how the word 'infinite' means something that goes on and on and never ends? Well, finite is the opposite – it means 'finished' or 'complete'. A finite verb is complete because it gives you all the information – it tells you when something was done, and also how many people did it.

Mm, sounds a bit strange. Let me see, how

can I explain it . . . Well, lots of verbs are complete just as they are. Like:

The polar bear **baked** the mulberry pie.

Sounds good. But what about this:

The polar bear **baking** the mulberry pie.

Say it out loud. There's something missing, isn't there? Something not quite right. What is it? Could it be just one little word?

The polar bear **is baking** the mulberry pie.

That's better! 'Is' is just a little word, but it's part of the verb that can often make it complete (or finite).

So now we know that the polar bear is baking that pie right at this moment. After all, if it happened yesterday we'd put in a different little word, 'was'.

The polar bear **was baking** the mulberry pie.

And if there was more than one polar bear involved at the time, we'd have to choose another word again:

The polar bears **were baking** the mulberry pie.

But really you should never have more than one polar bear in the kitchen at a time . . .

Not as Hard as It Looks

Sometimes the sorts of words you need to complete a verb are called 'auxiliary verbs', which means 'helping'. Some common ones are **am, is, are, was, were, has, have, will be, have been** – I'll stop there, you get the idea.

It probably sounds a bit complicated but really it's not so hard. If you're writing a sentence and you're wondering if the verb is finite or not, usually if you read it out loud you'll realise what's missing by listening to how it sounds.

After all, even quite little children use finite verbs in their sentences. Of course, if you asked a four-year-old, 'What's a finite verb?' they might answer, 'At my school I can hop on one leg' or something equally interesting. But just because they don't know how to explain it doesn't mean that they don't know how to use it!

Fragments

The Word Spy has gone inside?
Yes, to the darkest corner of the library.
All alone?
Sure was.

How many sentences are there here? Four. Four? Wait a minute. Only one of those sentences has a subject and a finite verb, and that's the first one. So how can those others be sentences?

Well, they're a special sort of sentence called 'fragments'. Fragments, of course, are what you find on the floor when you accidentally drop your auntie's favourite vase.

But there's another meaning. You will have seen it on word-processing programs. A wiggly line will appear under a sentence that is missing a verb, to remind you just in case you want to put one in.

Because, unlike your auntie's vase, the great thing about sentence fragments is you can put them back together again if you want to.

Has The Word Spy gone inside?
Yes, she has gone to the darkest corner of the library.
Was she all alone?
She sure was all alone.

When we speak, we use fragments all the time and we fill in the missing pieces with our minds. But writers sometimes deliberately write in fragments too, to create an effect.

In fact, a French novelist, Michel Thaler, wrote a whole novel, *The Train from Nowhere,* all in fragments, without a single verb at all!

What a strange idea. A story without any verbs. Not possible, surely. But then again, why not? (Hmm, not so hard after all.)

I Object!

The polar bear baked the **mulberry pie**.

Okay, if the polar bear is the subject, and baked is the finite verb, what's the mulberry pie? (Apart from being something delicious to eat with vanilla ice cream.) Ah, the mulberry pie is the 'object'.

You know what an object is. It's a thing. (What's that object sticking out of your school bag?) Like the subject, an object is usually a kind of noun. But what makes something an object is really what is being done to it.

The polar bear baked something. What did she bake? A mulberry pie. So the mulberry pie is the object.

If the polar bear was baking a banana muffin, then the object would be – yep, the banana muffin. And if the polar bear was baking your next-door neighbours, then the object would be, sadly for them, your next-door neighbours . . .

Order! Order!

You make decisions about subjects and objects all the time, even if you don't realise it. I bet you've played around with those little magnetic words people have on their fridge. You have to put them in some kind of order. The order you put them in can change the meaning of your sentence. Say you put the words like this:

The vulture scared Sally.

Sounds good. (Although maybe not for Sally.) The vulture is the subject and Sally is the object. But what happens if you turned it around?

Sally scared the vulture.

Aha! Now Sally is the subject and the vulture is the object and the sentence has a very different meaning. (Tsk tsk, bad Sally!)

In English, words usually go in this order: first, the subject, then the verb, then the object. But not always. In poems the word order is sometimes different because it might suit the rhythm or rhyme better.

And even in ordinary conversation people change the word order for all sorts of reasons. As The Word Spy's Auntie Fang would say:

'I like dogs. I admire cows. But chickens
I love.'

Yep, she sure loves those chickens. And do you remember Yoda in the *Star Wars* movies? He had an odd way of speaking sometimes with mixed-up word order. He'd say things like:

'Good relations with the Wookiees I have.'
'Never his mind on where he was.'
'Not if anything to say about it I have.'

Gosh. Imagine if Auntie Fang and Yoda ever met – what a weird conversation *that* would be!

Is It Me or You?

It's also useful to know about subjects and objects when you're using pronouns. Remember them? Those words that stand in for other nouns, like **I, you, he, she, it, we** and **they**.

Oh, and **me, him, her, us** and **them**. What? Ah, you see, that's the trick with pronouns. Unlike other nouns they can change, depending on whether they're the subject or the object.

The reason they change when other nouns don't is because they're leftovers. Not last night's baked beans, but leftovers from Old English. When English began, all nouns changed depending on whether they were the subject or the object. But over time, most of these changes faded away and the pronouns are just about the only ones we have left.

Have a look at this entry in The Word Spy's diary. Can you pick which pronouns are subjects and which ones are objects?

*I tapped my piano teacher on the shoulder. **She** asked **me** what was wrong. **I** told **her** that **I** was afraid to touch the piano keys, because a giant hairy spider was sitting on **them**.*

*'Should **I** try to remove **it**?' **I** asked my teacher, nervously. 'What if **it** attacks **us**?'*

*'**You** mustn't worry about **him**,' **she** told **me**, smiling. '**He** won't hurt **you**. **He**'s just my Uncle Andrew, being friendly.'*

Did you find them all? And I wonder if you spotted the pronouns that don't change, but are always the same. (If you said, 'it' and 'you', congratulations, you're right!)

Are you talking about me?

It's easy to get confused with pronouns, whether to use 'I' or 'me', or 'he' or 'him', for example. But I'll let you in on a secret. Read this:

Dorabel pushed me into the pool.

Great sentence. (If you can swim, that is.) But look what can happen if you throw my friend Yuki in too.

Dorabel pushed Yuki and I into the pool.

Hey! Hang on! Where did that 'I' come from? What happened to 'me'? There's no need to change the word just because Yuki turned up.

Here's the trick to make sure you get it right. Toss Yuki out of the sentence again. (Sorry, Yuki.) You wouldn't say 'Dorabel pushed I', would you? It sounds funny. So, okay, bring Yuki back:

Dorabel pushed Yuki and me into the pool.

Perfect!

It's Its, Isn't It?

Just while we're on the subject of tricky pronouns . . .

It.

What a great word. Remember Cousin Itt – that small hairy person on *The Addams Family*? He looked a lot of fun. But I'm afraid 'it' with one 't' can give you quite a headache!

It's all to do with the apostrophe. I'm sure you've learnt somewhere along the way that you put an apostrophe into a word to show something belongs to someone. Like 'The Word Spy's donkey' is just another way of writing 'the donkey of The Word Spy'.

So, if you were writing a story about a dog, and you wanted to say there was a fly on the end of the dog's nose, is this what you would write?

A fly was on the end of it's nose.

I know it looks as if you should, but actually, no. It seems silly, but you don't put in an apostrophe at all. Not before the 's' and not after the 's'. This is the only time we don't use an apostrophe to show belonging.

This is the way to write it:

A fly was on the end of its nose.

In fact, the ONLY time you have an apostrophe with the word 'its' is when it's short for 'it is'. The good news is that it's very easy to check. Just separate the 'it's' into 'it' and 'is' in your sentence, and see if it still makes sense:

A fly was on the end of it is nose.

Does it still make sense? No? Then get rid of that apostrophe. Go on, apostrophe, shoo! Get out of here!

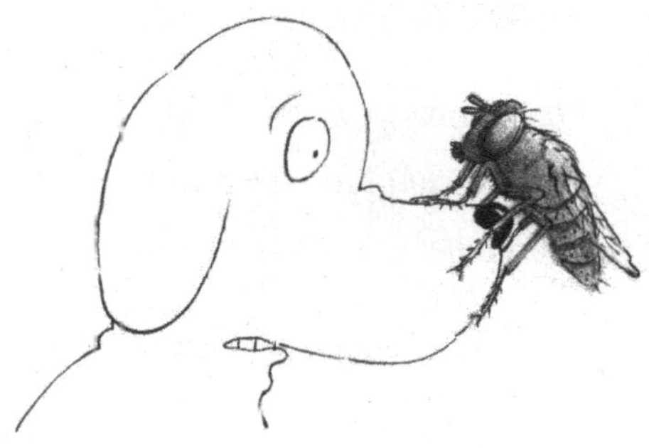

PS Think I'll go and watch *The Addams Family* now!

The word is spinning
Round your head . . .
A spoonerism*, please
Instead

Student: Look at that pretty little yellow canary over there!

Dr Spooner: Oh no. That's no canary, you fool, it's a vungry hultcher . . . Rick! Quun!

*A spoonerism? Gosh, back to The Word Spy!

6.

Nouns are like ice cream

Vanilla Choc-chip, Please

Like flavours of ice cream in an ice-cream parlour, there are all kinds of nouns. Maybe not strawberry, caramel or hokey-pokey, but other flavours just as interesting – proper nouns, count nouns, and those pesky little pronouns.

So come on, get out your spoon and chocolate sauce, and get tasting!

Being Proper

This one's easy. A 'proper' noun is simply a noun that starts with a capital letter. All the other nouns are 'common' nouns. See? I told you it was easy.

But wait a minute – what makes a noun proper? Why does it start with a capital letter? Ah, yes.

Okay, the point of a proper noun is that it's something or someone that's one of a kind. I bet one of the first nouns you ever wrote was a proper noun. Yep, that's right – your name. There's only one of you (let's hope so), so that's why your name is a proper noun and written with a capital at the beginning.

In the same way, the names of places are also proper nouns. There's only one Antarctica, and one Bangkok. Proper nouns are also one-off events in history like the French Revolution or the Great Vowel Shift (remember that from my first book, *The Word Spy*?). In English we also write the months and the days of the week as proper nouns, and the names of languages. The same goes for titles of books and brand names, like Weet-Bix or Crayola.

So proper nouns are one-of-a-kind nouns. All the other nouns, like mouse or sandwich or igloo or escalator or – um, I could go on like this for the rest of the book, actually, so I'll stop it right there – are common nouns.

This means when I say 'The Word Spy', you know exactly who I'm talking about. But if I said 'word spies', I'd mean a whole lot of them out there snooping away, and I'm not sure exactly who they are . . .

I'm not shouting

It would have been easier a few thousand years ago, when there was no such thing as a proper noun or a common noun because EVERYTHING WAS IN CAPITAL LETTERS. That's how writing began. Then gradually, as more and more people started writing, they made rounder smaller letters, which were easier to write. By the Middle Ages there were definite upper and lower case letters, but there were still no strict rules about which words should have capitals and which shouldn't. It took quite a few more hundred years for people to agree on that.

Look at these lines from one of the most famous documents in the world, written in 1776. There are capital letters all over the place – not to mention the strange spelling . . .

He is at this time transporting large Armies of foreign Mercenaries to compleat the works of death, desolation and tyranny, already begun with circumstances of Cruelty & perfidy scarcely paralleled in the most barbarous ages, and totally unworthy the Head of a civilized nation.

Gosh, what an annoying person. Are you wondering who it was? Well, this is from the Declaration of Independence, when the United States of America declared independence from Great Britain. And the person they are talking about is Britain's King George III!

But why am I proper?

By the way, have you ever wondered why we write the word 'I' with a capital letter, but not 'he' or 'she' or 'we' or 'you'? (Or me?) Historians think the reason is that the word 'I' in Old English was 'Ich', but over time the 'ch' dropped off. So all that was left was the 'I'. This was such a short word, printers wanted to make sure that people saw it properly in books, so they made it into a capital.

Can You Count?

Okay, so there are common nouns and proper nouns. But did you know there are also 'count nouns' and 'non-count' nouns? You've guessed it: a count noun is something you can count.

One giraffe, two giraffes, three giraffes, four giraffes – okay, okay, that's enough giraffes! We know you can count.

Most nouns are count nouns. But some nouns can't be counted. Take 'health'. One health, two healths, three – hey, that doesn't work. You can't have more than one health.

That's right. Which is why 'health' is a non-count noun. You can't make it into a plural. English has quite a few non-count nouns. Like cutlery, and furniture. And dust. And water. Can you think of some more?

Only many

When The Word Spy was at her cousin Alyosha's for dinner the other night, she heard his grandmother say sharply:

> 'Alyosha, mind your manner and eat your green!'
>
> Alyosha moaned back:
>
> 'But Grandmama, you have given me an oodle of brussel sprout to eat.'

Hmm, there's something funny there. Can you mind your manner? Or eat a green or an oodle?

These are actually kinds of nouns that are only found in the plural. You can't have only one of them. They go by the name *plurale tantum*, which is Latin for 'only plural'. Often only-plural nouns are for things that have two halves joined together. Think of 'scissors' or 'trousers'. You can't say, 'Please pass me a scissor,' or 'Today I'm going to wear my lime green trouser.'

And what about something you might need at a barbecue to turn the sausages over? Or a tool you could use to get a splinter out of your finger? (Ouch.)

Collective Nouns

Now we come to 'collective' nouns, the special words for when you have a group of something. You know, a **flock** of sheep, or a **mob** of kangaroos, or a **herd** of stampeding guinea pigs. (Eeek!)

Some collective nouns we use a lot. But others are rare and pretty strange. Ever heard anyone talk about a **leap** of leopards or a **glaring** of cats?

Many of these unusual collective nouns come from a book published in the 15th century called *The Book of St Albans*. The writer listed (and probably invented) a whole lot of them, and people have had fun inventing them ever since. Like a **pity** of prisoners, a **murder** of crows, a **blush** of boys. Or a **float** of crocodiles, a **skulk** of foxes, or a **glint** of goldfish . . .

It's a lot of fun making up collective nouns. Have a go yourself – they could be for groups of anything at all. You could start with these:

* mobile phones
* teddy bears
* wombats
* lemonade bottles

A Noun in Disguise

There's a kind of noun that sometimes makes people scratch their heads and frown because it looks as if it's something else.

Tolbert adores **skipping**.

Hmm. Now, because 'skipping' ends in 'ing', you might think it's part of a verb. It looks exactly the same, after all.

Tolbert is **skipping**.

In that sentence, 'skipping' is part of the verb. But remember how I said that it's what the words are actually doing in their sentences that's the important thing? With 'Tolbert adores skipping', the word 'skipping' is really a noun and 'adores' is the verb. It's easy to tell if you add something else:

Tolbert adores **skipping** and **llamas**.

Both 'skipping' and 'llamas' are objects of the sentence. (What a strange child that Tolbert sounds.) So the word 'skipping' there is being used as a noun. It's a 'noun verb', AKA a 'gerund'.

It can happen the other way round too, by the way. Nouns turn into verbs from time to time. Like, 'Who wants to party?' or 'I'm going to shampoo my hair.'

Can you think of some more?

Um, Is That Chair a Girl or a Boy?

In English this is an easy question to answer. We don't think of a noun like a chair being male or female. We just think it's a chair. Isn't it?

But in lots of other languages ordinary nouns like 'chair' have a gender. This means they can be masculine or feminine or even neuter (neither one or the other). For example, in German a knife is neuter, a fork is feminine and a spoon is masculine. Think about that when you sit down at the dinner table tonight!

Messer (neuter) – knife
Gabel (feminine) – fork
Löffel (masculine) – spoon

We might think that's very peculiar, but actually when English began our nouns had genders too. For example, a stone was masculine, while a gift was feminine, and a house was neuter. But over time we just gave up on it (too complicated!) and now we only have gender for things that are actually male and female in a biological sort of way, like 'he' and 'she', 'widow' and 'widower', or 'lion' and 'lioness'.

Of course, grammar books will tell you that the gender of a noun in a language like French or German has nothing to do with the gender of a person. It's just a way of putting nouns into groups. It doesn't really mean French people think of a chair as a 'girl' just because it's feminine. People who grow up speaking languages with genders probably don't think about it at all, because it seems natural to them.

Maybe it does mean something though. Have a look around the classroom at the chairs, tables, books, pens, computers, whatever you can see. If they had to be masculine or feminine, what would you choose each one to be?

I wonder why . . .

What word is this?
I hear you cry
A number puzzle's
Worth a try

7.15.12.4.6.9.19.8
(Hint: What has 26 letters in it?)

7. Verbs are like goldfish

Something Gold and Gleaming

Verbs are fascinating, but very mysterious. Trying to understand how verbs work is like trying to catch a goldfish with your bare fingers. They're slippery and shiny; they can hide in the dark reeds underwater then suddenly shoot upwards to the surface and give you a shock.

Let's get our nets out and see if we can catch a few!

Too Much Tension

Did you know that verbs can get tense? Very tense, actually. But don't worry. For a verb, the word 'tense' doesn't mean quite the same thing as it does for us.

When The Word Spy is tense, she bites her fingernails and scrunches up her face and her eyes start to pop out. But for a verb, a tense is all about *when* something happened.

Here is the 'present' tense, something that's happening now:

The watermelon **is falling** on my head.

Here is the 'past' tense, something that has already happened:

The watermelon **fell** on my head.

Or if you are a fortune teller, here is the 'future' tense, something that hasn't happened yet:

The watermelon **will fall** on my head.

(Hey, who's throwing all these watermelons?)

Once upon a time

The past tense is the tense you use most often when you are writing a story. Maybe this is because stories often begin with someone telling something that actually happened to them. I mean, if a watermelon really did fall on your head yesterday and you wanted to tell your best friend, you would probably tell it in the past tense. Like, 'Wow, yesterday, there I was, sitting there minding my own business, when this giant watermelon fell on my head!' So when you make up an entirely imaginary story, it seems natural to use the past tense.

But you don't *have* to write your stories in the past tense. I bet you've read books written in the present tense. Lots of picture books are written like that – you know, 'Here is the bear. Here is the green jelly. Oh no! The green jelly is chasing the bear! Run, bear, run!' The present tense can make a story seem more exciting, as though it's happening at the same time that you're reading it.

Some writers even like to mix their tenses up, to really confuse you. A very famous book called *Bleak House*, by the English writer Charles Dickens, is written partly in the present tense and partly in the past tense. And before you ask, yep, there have even been books written in the future tense. Here's the first sentence of *A Very Private Life* by Michael Frayn:

> *Once upon a time there will be a*
> *little girl called Uncumber.*

Now, I wonder what happened to Uncumber? Or should I say, I wonder what *will* happen to her?

Finding Your Voice

Verbs don't only get tense, they also have a voice.

What – verbs can speak? Not exactly. In English, verbs can have two different voices. One is called the 'active' voice, and the other the 'passive' voice.

People are sometimes described as active. That means they run around a lot and get plenty of things done. Other people are more passive – they like lying down and getting other (active?) people to do things for them. This is sort of how it works in a sentence too.

> The black swan **is eating** an upside-down pineapple cake.

You can see that the swan is doing all the eating in this sentence, so here 'is eating' is in the active voice. Now have a look at it in the passive voice:

> The upside-down pineapple cake **is being eaten** by the black swan.

The upside-down pineapple cake is 'being eaten' and that's passive. Sigh. If it had only been a bit more active, it might have got up and run away . . .

Being scientific

There are all sorts of reasons for using the passive voice instead of the active voice. It's often found in science reports to make something sound as though nobody's personal feelings are getting into what's being said. You're just told what was done to things, not necessarily who did it. Like this:

The liquid was poured into the glass beaker.
It was then heated to boiling point.

Here's a more active version:

I poured the liquid into the beaker and
I heated it to boiling point. Suddenly I felt
nervous and I thought, Oh no! It's going to
explode! I ran screaming from the room.

Hmm, not very scientific – but definitely more exciting!

Who dunnit?

Sometimes people use the passive voice when they want to cover up the fact that they don't know who actually did something. Imagine you were a busy journalist, and you found a suspiciously empty pie plate with a few crumbs and purple juice on it, but you just didn't have time to find out who had eaten the pie. No problem. You could just write this passive headline:

SHOCK! MULBERRY PIE HAS BEEN EATEN!

The passive is also handy when you *do* know who has done something but you don't want anyone else to know. For example, if you were an alligator, and your mother came home from work and flopped down in a chair and said, 'Bring me a piece of mulberry pie, please darling', you might hang your head and mumble:

'Um, the mulberry pie has been eaten . . .'

then quickly run out to play in the back yard. Who do you think ate it?

Are You in a Good Mood?

Let's hope so. Then you'll be ready to hear that verbs don't just get tense, they also have moods. Yep, they're pretty moody things altogether.

The most common mood is called the 'indicative' mood (or sometimes the 'declarative'). You use it when you're simply declaring something in a straightforward way. Most verbs we use are like this.

I **jumped** into the mud bath.
He **licks** the ice cream.
She **will give** the piglet a surprise.

And That's an Order

Then there's the 'imperative' mood. The name for this mood comes from a Latin word *imperatum*, a command. It's a good name because you use the imperative mood when you are commanding someone to do something. Like:

'**Jump** into the mud bath!'

We use imperatives quite a lot, and some people use them all the time. An army officer, for example. If you were in charge of a troop of soldiers, you probably wouldn't get far if just before a battle you stood up and said:

> 'Um, I was just wondering, would you soldiers mind getting up now and putting your guns on your shoulders? And then you could possibly run down that little hill over there, I mean, if you feel like it. And I'd really like you to hide behind that tree at the bottom of the hill when the enemy comes. Is that okay with everyone?'

How do you think you would rewrite that speech in the imperative? Come on! Think! GET ON WITH IT!

I Wish I May, I Wish I Might

Now we come to the 'subjunctive' mood. This one is for when you want to talk about something that might happen or could happen or should happen or that you wish would happen. (Phew!)

Like this:

I wish you **would jump** into the mud bath. Do you imagine that you **might jump** into the mud bath?

Or:

May blessings be upon your children's grandchildren, **should you decide** to jump into the mud bath.

The famous Danish philosopher Søren Kierkegaard loved the subjunctive mood. He thought it was a very good mood for writers, full of imaginary wishes and hopes:

One should be able to write a whole novel in which the present tense subjunctive were the invisible soul, as light is for painting.

Gosh!

On one condition

The subjunctive is different to what's called the 'conditional'. Conditional verbs also come with words like 'if', but they are not imagining what things would be like 'if only' something happened. They are saying what will really happen! Here's a sentence with a conditional verb:

> If I put my sunhat in the freezer, it will freeze.

Now that's a fact. Hat in freezer – result: one frozen hat. (Could be handy on a hot day.) Compare that to a subjunctive sentence:

> If I put my sunhat in the freezer, then my father might mistake it for a frozen chop and cook it up for dinner.

Erk! Let's hope that stays in the world of the imagination . . .

From Here to Infinity

Now for some good news. There's a kind of verb that has no tense, voice or mood. Wow! Sounds fantastic. So, what is it?

It's called the 'infinitive'. Here's what it looks like:

The buffalo started **to giggle**.
The baby wants **to stand** on her head.
The chewing gum began **to harden**.

As you can see, the infinitive often comes after another verb and usually contains the word 'to'. But sometimes it's even simpler, without the 'to':

I can **count**.
She thought she could **fly**.

Ah, yes, those infinitives. Infinitely loveable!

Give Me My Money Back

By the way, after all this verby stuff, don't worry if you find yourself making mistakes with verbs. Because did you know that some verbs in English are officially defective?

'Defective' means there's something wrong. Defective verbs are ones that have got some parts missing. Take 'must', for example. Must is defective because it's missing a future tense. You can't say 'I will must.' You have to look around and find other words, like 'I will have to.' It's the same with 'can'. It doesn't have a future either. You have to say 'I will be able.'

If you bought a wind-up duck at the toy shop that didn't work once you got it home, you could go back to the shop and slam it on the counter and say, 'Excuse me! This duck is defective.' The bad news is that you can't do that with English verbs. You just have to put up with them.

I demand my money back!

If seeking words
Makes you feel sick
It's time to try an
A-cros-tic!

I swim round lakes
And ponds a lot. I'm –
Sometimes
White
And sometimes
Not . . .
What am I?

8.

What do words mean, anyway?

Ever Had a Green Idea?

Okay, we've just been talking lots and lots about how to make sentences work. But now I have to tell you the bad news. The odd thing about language is that even if you say or write a perfect sentence without a single mistake, it can still make no sense at all!

??

You don't believe me? All right, read this:

Colourless green ideas sleep furiously.

Now that is a truly excellent sentence. Look at all those parts of speech. Hmm, two adjectives, a noun, a finite verb AND an adverb. Full marks. Only one problem. It doesn't mean anything . . .

A Horse Is a Horse, of Course

The sentence about the sleepy green ideas was written by Noam Chomsky (remember him from Chapter 3?). He wrote it on purpose to show that meaning something is not as easy as it seems.

So how DO you make words actually mean something? Ah, people have been wondering about that question for thousands of years.

Someone who thought a lot about it was the philosopher Plato, who lived in Athens, Greece, in the 5th century BC. He was a pupil of a very famous teacher named Socrates. Plato wrote down lots of the conversations that Socrates had with his pupils. (Imagine if you wrote down everything *your* teacher said!)

Here's a part of one of those conversations, all about what words mean. One of Socrates' students, Hermogenes, is saying that a word, a name for something, doesn't have a 'true' meaning. It's only what people agree to mean at the time.

HERMOGENES: *Socrates, in my opinion, any name you give to something is the right one. If you change it and give another, the new name is as correct as the old.*

SOCRATES: *I dare say you're right, Hermogenes. Let's see. You mean the name of each thing is only that which anybody agrees to call it?*

HERMOGENES: *That is my notion.*

SOCRATES: *Well, now. Suppose I call a man a horse, or a horse a man. You mean to say that a man will be rightly called a horse by me, and rightly called a man by the rest of the world? And a horse again would be rightly called a man by me, and a horse by the world?*

Phew! You can say that again . . .

According to the Big Egg

As you can see, it can all get pretty complicated once you stop and think about it. On the opposite page is another interesting conversation, this time between a little girl called Alice and the celebrity egg, Humpty Dumpty. It comes from a book called *Through the Looking Glass, and What Alice Found There* by Lewis Carroll.

Alice and Humpty are also arguing about the true meaning of words.

'I don't know what you mean by "glory",' Alice said.

Humpty Dumpty smiled contemptuously.

'Of course you don't – till I tell you. I meant "there's a nice knock-down argument for you!"'

'But "glory" doesn't mean "a nice knock-down argument",' Alice objected.

'When I use a word,' Humpty Dumpty said, in rather a scornful tone, 'it means just what I choose it to mean – neither more nor less.'

'The question is,' said Alice, 'whether you CAN make words mean so many different things.'

'The question is,' said Humpty Dumpty, 'which is to be master – that's all.'

Looks like, according to Humpty, what a word means depends on what *he* wants it to mean – and it may not be what's in the dictionary! He thinks he can make up his own rules. (I bet you know someone who plays Monopoly like that.)

In the famous words of Inigo Montoya in *The Princess Bride*:

'I do not think it means what you think it means.'

The Words They Are a'Changing

One of the problems with words is that they're not solid things. They can start off meaning one thing, and, on their wordy journey through time and place, begin to mean something else. It can happen so gradually that each person using the word is probably not aware they're using it slightly differently each time.

Take the word 'nice'. A thousand years ago, if you said someone was nice it meant they were stupid. As hundreds of years passed, 'nice'

gradually changed in meaning, and started to mean someone who was a bit fussy. By the 18th century people were also using it for something that was pleasant. And nowadays it means, well, 'nice'.

So it can be important to know when something you're reading was written. After all, if a teacher hundreds of years ago said to a pupil, 'Your test result is tremendous!' it meant something quite different to what your teacher would mean today. 'Tremendous' used to be a word for something so horrible that it made you tremble with fear. (Aaaagh – put that test away!)

Changes in the meaning of words can happen quickly as well as slowly. Some words come to mean different things in a matter of a few years. Do you think the two people talking on the next page are really understanding each other?

Young person: That singer is so sick.

Old person: Really? Perhaps he should see a doctor.

Young person: He doesn't need a doctor. He's wicked!

Old person: Dear, dear. I'm sorry to hear that.

Young person: Don't worry about it. It's cool.

Old person: Hmm, better put your cardigan on then.

Young person: ???!!!!?????

Old person: Speak up, sonny, I can't hear you!

Wild Geese

It's not only single words that change meaning and get us scratching our heads. English is full of strange and funny expressions we use in our everyday speech without stopping to think why. Some of them have fascinating beginnings.

You would have heard people say that someone is going to 'turn over a new leaf', to mean they are going to try to behave better. When The Word Spy first heard that, she immediately imagined a nice green leaf that had fallen from a tree. But in fact it comes from an old-fashioned word for the page of a book. So when you turn over a new leaf, it's like having a nice clean page to write on.

Another funny one is 'lick into shape'. Mostly you hear scary sports teachers saying this, when they stare at you all huddled at the edge of the oval. It means they're going to get you fit and ready – or else! Amazingly, the expression comes from a belief going back hundreds of years about baby bears. People thought that when bears were born they were shapeless lumps, and they had to be 'licked into shape' by their mother. Have you ever seen a mother dog licking her newborn puppies clean? They do look pretty blobby.

For other expressions it's harder to discover where they first started. Take to 'break the ice'. We use this to mean a way of getting people who don't know each other relaxed and happy at a party or meeting. It *may* have come from the time when people had to break the ice that formed on the top of a well to be able to get any water out of it. Or it could have come from the need for ships to break the ice on the surface of the sea in very cold places before sailing through. Nobody knows for sure.

And finally, 'it takes the cake'. Cakes have been traditional prizes for thousands of years, but this expression seems to have become most popular in the United States in the 19th century. There was a kind of dance competition called the 'cakewalk' and the prize was – you've guessed it – a cake!

Here are a few more expressions in English that you might have wondered about. See if you can discover where they came from.

* Beat around the bush
* Leave no stone unturned
* Raining cats and dogs
* Swan song
* Throw in the towel
* Wild goose chase

Bad Language

Another way you can see how words change their meaning, depending on the situation and how they're used, is to look at BAD language. You know, like:

%&*@#&$&#%*#!!!!!

If you're a comic-book reader, you'll have seen this sort of thing. All the little symbols on the top of the typewriter are put together in a row to show that the person is swearing. You don't need the actual words – you get the idea!

In English, swearing is sometimes called 'four-letter words' or 'expletives' or 'cursing'. And have you ever heard an older person say, 'Excuse my French'? They actually mean 'Oops, sorry for swearing.'

'To swear' also means 'to take an oath'. An oath is a serious promise, usually made in the name of God. Early swear words were based on religion. Religious words are often thought of as taboo – a word for things you are not supposed to talk about. Religion can be a big taboo, and so are other things. (I'm sure you can think of a few!)

This is where the mystery of the human personality comes in. When someone is angry or shocked or anxious about something, to relieve their tension they might say a taboo word and woooh! suddenly they feel a bit better. That's why swearing is often found in jokes and comedy, which relieve tension as well. The meaning of the word is the effect it has on your emotions.

Now, some people swear a lot. They don't think of swear words as being much different to any other words and they use them all the time. But other people never swear, and they're not used to hearing or reading swearing. If someone swears at them they can become distressed or frightened.

That's why there are rules about swearing on television or on the radio, because you don't know what sort of person may be listening. It's a kind of respect. Respect is also the reason why there are some places you are not supposed to swear, like a court house, or people you are not supposed to swear in front of, like your teacher or a police officer.

That's when you need the 'BEEEEEEP' over the top of what someone is saying – expletive deleted!

What is the word?
If you don't know
Then try to solve the rhyme
Below

My first is in hob
But not in hot
My second's in neat
But not in not . . .
My third is in neat as well, you know
And my last is in fore
But not in foe.
What am I?
(Grrrrrrrrrrrrrrrrrrrrrrrrrrrrrrrrr!)

9.

Words, words, words

In the Beginning Was . . . a Word

Words are always changing, as you can see. How can we keep track of them all?

There's a special word for the study of where words come from, how they change in meaning and maybe where they're going: etymology. (No, not entomology, that's the study of insects – very interesting, but quite a different thing altogether!)

Etymos means 'true' in Ancient Greek, and *logos* means 'word'. Etymologists are people who look through books, poems, government records, emails, websites, advertisements, songs, inscriptions, television programs, radio shows, films, letters and whatever else they can find to try and work out where a word truly began.

Bitter-water-mud cake

Word spies just love etymology. Some big dictionaries will give the etymology of a word you are looking up as well as the meaning. So if you find the word 'chocolate' in a dictionary like that, after it tells you that it's delicious sweet stuff made of cocoa, it might say something like:

from Nahuatl chocolatl, *meaning 'bitter water'*

Nahuatl is a language spoken in Mexico, which is where chocolate originally came from. (Glad they started adding sugar and milk!)

Or you might look up the word 'muscle' and find out that it comes from the Latin word *musculus*, which means 'little mouse'. This is because people thought their muscles looked like little mice bouncing up their arm under their skin. (Eeek!)

Discovering things like this is what makes etymology endlessly intriguing. You can even get special etymological dictionaries and websites that are completely devoted to the history of words. You'll be amazed at what you can find out. It's like looking at a building and finding out who built it and why, or eating a delicious stew or curry and discovering what ingredients are inside that make it taste that particular way . . .

Still in the Dark

Sometimes when you look up a word in the dictionary it will say something like 'origin obscure' or 'origin unknown'. This means that etymologists haven't been able to work out where the word began. 'Obscure' comes from the Latin word *obscurus*, meaning 'in the dark'.

How does this happen? Well, one of the problems is that to trace the beginnings of many, many words, etymologists have to rely on things that are written down, like books, newspapers, diaries and letters. Nowadays we have lots of places where we keep records of spoken words, like films, CDs, mp3s, videos, YouTube and more. But there's nobody alive from, say, the 17th century, to tell us how words were being used in everyday conversation then. Some of these words are hiding in the shadows, not letting any of their secrets out. Read this obscure story which uses quite a few words with murky beginnings. Have you got a dictionary? See if you can find which words I'm talking about.

An Obscure Story

Once upon a time a fussy squid was having a snooze after guzzling a jam sandwich. He was flabbergasted, not to mention puzzled, when a bloke surfed by on a freak wave and landed higgledy-piggledy in a jumble on the floor.

'You nincompoop!' cried the squid. 'My home is in turmoil!'

'Don't get in a tiff, tootsie,' bantered the bloke. 'I'll toddle off before you have a tantrum.'

If in Doubt (Don't) Make It Up

When nobody really knows where a word started, it's natural for people to wonder about it. And in all that wondering, it's easy to make connections that aren't really there. This is how we end out with what are called 'folk' etymologies. These are explanations that sound convincing, but usually aren't true. You can see how it happens. Words can sometimes seem connected when actually they have nothing much to do with each other. I'll show you what I mean.

The word 'phony' means 'fake'. Now, sometimes 'funny' means fake – like in the expressions 'funny money' and 'funny business'. So some people have thought that 'phony' comes from 'funny' because they sound similar.

But wait! The word 'phony' also looks like 'phone'. Another theory is that there was a kind of telephone trick, where robbers would ring someone up and say there was an emergency down the street. Then, while the person rushed off in a panic, the robber would go and break into their house. So it was a 'phony' (fake) trick!

Both these explanations sound more or less possible. But according to etymologists, these are folk etymologies and they are not true. The word phony actually comes from an Irish Gaelic word, *faine*, a kind of ring. As time passed, this turned into *fawney*, meaning a shiny fake ring, which then changed its spelling into *phony* and came to mean anything fake.

Most of the time false etymologies are

innocent mistakes. But sometimes people make up a fake etymology on purpose, maybe for fun, or to trick someone. The problem is, once a very convincing fake explanation gets around, it's hard to get people not to believe it.

OK *okay?*

'Okay' is a good example of this. Okay first appeared in the language in the United States more than a hundred years ago. What a successful word it has been! Yet nobody really knows how it started. If you look it up in the dictionary or on the internet, you will find dozens of suggestions. Some of them are *almost* believable . . .

Here are a few of the explanations of okay. The Word Spy has added an extra silly one she invented herself. Can you guess which it is?

* It stands for 'orl korrect' – a misspelling of 'all correct'.
* It comes from the Ancient Greek letters Omega and Khi, which were used as a magic spell repeated twice to get rid of fleas.

* It's a shortened version of 'okapi', a kind of giraffe that nods a lot.
* It comes from a Native American word *okeh* meaning 'okay'.
* It comes from the Scottish expression 'och-aye'.
* It was used in a telegram during a war, 0K, meaning Zero Killed.

Okay, okay, that's enough – please!

(Whisper: Did you guess the one I made up? I'll give you hint: Look up in the air next time you're at the zoo.)

The False Etymology Game

There's a great game based on making up false etymologies. It's sometimes called The Dictionary Game, Fictionary or Balderdash. You can play versions of it online, and it's played on radio and television shows in different forms and languages all over the world.

Here's one way you can play it with your friends. You need a pretty big dictionary and at least four people, each with a pen and paper.

The person who is 'in' opens the dictionary and picks out a very very very unusual word that they are sure nobody will have heard of. (If anyone has heard of it, they have to admit it, and another word will be picked.)

Then everyone writes down a definition of the strange word. The person who is 'in' writes down the dictionary definition, but everyone else has to make something up. They hand over their definitions to the person who is 'in', who shuffles them up and reads each one aloud. All the players (except for the person who is 'in') have to say which definition they think comes from the dictionary. You score a point if you pick the dictionary definition. You also get a point for each person who picked your invented definition! This means you have fooled them.

Say the word picked was 'nutation'. On the next page are some definitions of this word. Which one do you think is the dictionary definition?

Nutation:	*A state of insanity that results from having eaten too many peanuts. See also 'nutty'.*
Nutation:	*A computer term for new developments in software; derived from 'nu' and 'mutation'.*
Nutation:	Nodding of the head, from the Latin, nutatio, nodding.
Nutation:	*A special day of national celebration when all the inhabitants of a country go about in the nude.*

Did you pick the right one? You'll have to go to the dictionary to find out!

Another word?
Please, that's enough!
Pig Latin is much*
Better stuff

I-ay inkth-ay ereth-ay is-ay
omethings-ay rawlingc-ay up-ay
our-y-ay leeves-ay. Um-ay, it-ay
ooksl-ay ikel-ay a-ay ousem-ay!

** Don't know any pigs? Or Latin?*
The Word Spy will reveal all . . .

10. Words wanted — dead or alive!

R.I.P. (Rest in Peace)

I'm warning you, I may get a bit emotional now. I'm about to tell you something very sad. Have you got a hanky? (A tissue will do.) Right, here goes. Sometimes you might see a word in the dictionary that is marked 'obsolete' or 'obs' for short. And, I'm sorry to say, obsolete is just a polite way of saying:

DEAD.

Yes, obsolete words are words that nobody uses anymore. They are deadibones. They used to be alive and kicking, but somehow people stopped saying them and they died.

Get a Haircut!

Take the word 'jagged'. It means something that's been cut very roughly. If you look it up in a dictionary, you will see that it comes from an obsolete word *jaggen*, which meant 'to cut'. But nowadays nobody says, 'Can you pass the scissors? I want to jaggen out this picture of a glow-worm.'

Nope, jaggen is well and truly buried. There are lots and lots of words deep down in the grave with jaggen. It's a pity, because some of those obsolete words are fantastic. When The Word Spy was at school she had a book of obsolete words. She liked them so much she used to put them into her stories. (Her poor teacher never quite knew what she was talking about!)

Hey, why don't you throw a few obsolete English words in next time you write something? Here are some to get you started. See if you can put them into a story. 'Something was coming usward from the welkin . . .'

* dern – dark
* moffle – to muck something up
* neesing – sneezing
* queechy – shaking
* sottish – silly
* swink – to work
* usward – towards us
* welkin – the sky
* whingle – complain
* And don't forget: forswunk – worn out from too much swinking!

Close to the Grave

In the dictionary you may also find words marked 'archaic', or 'arch' for short. Archaic means very old. Old, but not quite dead yet!

If a word is archaic, it's not used in everyday language, but we can usually recognise it and know what it means. You know, things like 'thee' and 'thine' for 'you' and 'yours', or 'methinks' for 'I think', or 'zounds!' for 'gosh!' Writers sometimes use archaic words when they want to give the reader a feeling of the past. You'll often see them in historical stories.

But there are other reasons a writer might want to use archaic words. The great American novelist John Steinbeck wrote a book called *Tortilla Flat*, set in California just after World War One. The characters speak to each other like this:

'Thy mode of living keeps all thy friends uneasy.'

I don't suppose anyone in California ever really spoke like that! So why did he do it? Well, one of Steinbeck's favourite books was *The Death of Arthur* by Sir Thomas Malory, all about King Arthur and the Knights of the Round Table, written in England in the 15th century. Steinbeck loved the way the knights behaved and spoke to each other. He wanted to create the same feeling in the characters of his own book, even though they lived at the other end of the world hundreds of years later.

Newborn Words

All right everybody, put your hankies away. We've had enough of all these dead and dying words. It's time for some happy news for a change. Because new words are being born all the time! Hurray! There's even a special name for them, *neologisms*, from the Ancient Greek meaning 'new word'.

Human beings seem to make up new words as naturally as breathing. Lots of neologisms come from technology, particularly from computers and the internet. These words describe new things for which no other word exists. Things like 'cyberspace', 'netiquette', 'phishing', 'twitter' – I'm sure you can think of lots more. Other neologisms come from television, music, jokes and famous personalities – words like 'bling', 'd'oh', 'supermodel', 'ecotourism'.

Like baby turtles on a beach, thousands of neologisms are born every year, but, alas, most of them die young. Few survive long enough to make it to the dictionary. We use them for a bit then we forget about them. Somehow they just don't catch on.

People who compile dictionaries make decisions about which new words they will include. A word has to have been in use for several years in plenty of places before they will list it. Like etymologists, dictionary compilers are word spies, too. They look for words everywhere – in television, radio, websites, books, emails, chat rooms, movies, songs, newspapers, magazines, gravestones, advertisements, annual reports, text messages, graffiti – in other words, wherever WORDS are found.

Be careful, they might be sitting behind you on the bus, listening to find out if you are using any new words!

Googol google googly

We all know what it means to google something. But imagine if you had been asleep for 20 years, like Rip Van Winkle, and then woke up. You might find it very strange if someone said they were going to google you. In fact, you might run straight back to the mountains to hide! Especially if they said they were going to text you, too . . .

There are a few googlish words out there – not just google but also 'googol' and even 'googly'. Let's start with googol. The word googol was a neologism invented by a nine-year-old boy.

An American mathematician, Edward Kasner, asked his nephew Milton to think of a name for a very long number, and that's what he came up with. Googol means the number one, followed by a hundred zeros.

10000000000000000000000000000000000
00000000000000000000000000000000000000
0000000000000000000000000000

His uncle then went on to invent the word 'googolplex', which is the number one followed by a googol of zeros. (I don't think I'll try writing that one out!)

The company Google adapted this lovely googolish word when they named themselves, because of the googol-load of information that's out there on the world wide web.

And googly? That's an Australian word for a funny way to bowl a ball in cricket so that it spins in a different direction to how it normally would. Where does the word come from? Mm, I'd say 'origin obscure'...

Serendipity

Ah, serendipity! What a lovely word. It sounds like a serene dip in a lake in the warm sunshine, with a butterfly wafting in the air above. At a London Festival of Literature poll for the most popular English word of all time, serendipity came out number one. (Quidditch came second.)

Serendipity actually means a situation when you discover good things when you're not out looking for them. It was a neologism invented in the 18th century by the eccentric English writer Horace Walpole. He came up with it from a story about the island of 'Serendip', another name for the beautiful island of Sri Lanka.

'I once read a silly fairy tale called The Three Princes of Serendip: *as their highnesses travelled, they were always making discoveries, by accident and sagacity, of things which they were not in quest of.'*

Horace Walpole loved making up new words. Another of his inventions was 'betweenity', to describe something that was between one thing and another – like:

> The betweenity of the sliced banana contained strawberry ice cream.

(Yum!) Another was 'triptology', the tendency to say things three times, which he thought was a very annoying habit, habit, habit. (Do you know any triptologists?)

And can you find the words he made up to describe his garden in this letter to a friend?

> *. . . these three years you have seen it only in winter: it is now in the height of its greenth, blueth (and) gloomth.*

Was that thunder?

Sometimes a writer will make up a word especially for something they are writing, and they don't really expect anyone else to use it. These are called 'nonce' words, from Old English meaning 'for a special occasion'.

You've seen nonce words. Think of Dr Seuss, with 'sneedle', 'glump', 'blurp', or Lewis Carroll, with 'jabberwocky', 'beamish', 'slithy'; Roald Dahl with 'snozzcumber', 'squiggle', 'humplecrimp'.

James Joyce was an Irish writer who loved nonce words. His book *Finnegans Wake* must surely have the most nonce words of all. Look at this crazy word he made up for the sound of a thunderclap (Can you say it out loud?):

BABABADALGHARAGHTAKAM-
MINARRONNKONNBRONNTON-
NERONNTUONNTHUNNTROVAR-
RHOUNAWNSKAWNTOOHOOHOO-
RDENENTHURNUK!

Well, you can see why that was a word you'd use only once . . .

Make Your Own Neologism

So now it's your turn. Why don't you invent a brand-new word? But how? Let's see.

Here's one way to do it. When Horace Walpole made up the word 'nincompoophood', first he took a word he already knew – 'nincompoop'. Then he made a new one by adding the ending 'hood'. Ta-da! Brand-new word.

'Hood' is something called a suffix, which means the letters that we put on the ends of words to make different meanings. So, if you add 'hood' to the word 'child' it makes 'childhood' – the time you are a child. So it follows that nincompoophood is the time you are a nincompoop. And caramelmilkshakehood is the time you are a caramel milkshake.

You can also make a neologism by adding a prefix, which is something fastened or fixed before a word. The prefix *mega* means 'big'. So if someone offers you a megaburger, you know you'll need a megaplate to put it on. *Multi*, on the other hand, means 'many'. So if your friend tells you that his cat had seven kittens, you could say, 'Congratulations! You are now a *multikitten* family.'

Here's a list of prefixes and suffixes you can use to make your own brand-new words. Go on. Let your words go wild!

Prefixes	Suffixes
co-	-ation
dis-	-ful
ex-	-ism
mal-	-itis
maxi-	-ity
mini-	-less
mis-	-ness
multi-	-lessness (!)
ultra-	-ship

Call that a word?
It's just a sham!
Let's have another
Anagram.

WRECKJAYBOB

11. The magical act of writing

Could You Write That Down?

Spies, we are nearly at the end of our journey. The time has gone so quickly, and we've passed through so many remarkable and wonderful places. But before we go home, I really want us to explore together one of the most astonishing marvels of all – the magical world of writing.

Remember when you learnt to write? It wasn't easy. You had to learn the letters of the alphabet. Then you had to find out how to put them together in words and how to spell. Then you had to learn how to use full stops and commas, and how to put the sentences into paragraphs.

Gee, what a lot of trouble – it was much easier to learn to speak! But you see, writing and speaking are quite different things when you think about it. Next time you're sitting in the playground with a couple of friends, try writing down what they are saying, word for word. (You'll have to be able to write very quickly.) What you end out with will be very different to a conversation you might read between two characters in a book.

This is because when you write a conversation between two people in a story, you usually cut out the boring bits, and the repetitions. You finish all the unfinished sentences. You put in punctuation. You make sentences, short or long. You put in paragraphs. You turn the language that you learnt through speaking into something else – writing.

Humans have developed so many different writing skills over thousands of years, from when the very first writing began back in at least 4000 BC. (If you want to know more about the history of writing, look in *The Word Spy*.) And ways of writing change and evolve with every passing day. Nowadays we can write everywhere – not just with pen and paper, but with computers, mobile phones, even with aeroplanes high up in the sky.

But what did people use all those thousands of years ago, when writing first began and they didn't have any of those things? Well, they used what they *did* have. They carved in rocks or drew on wood with burnt sticks or with their hands dipped in coloured mud. They made marks in the earth or in soft clay and they made brushes and pens out of bones, reeds and feathers. They made ink and paint out of oils mixed with earth, plants and shells. They wrote on bark, animal skins, silk and leaves.

If you could write on it or with it, they did. And all the time, new technologies were being discovered to make writing easier.

Poison Pencils

Like pencils. Remember how proud you were when you got your first pencil so you could learn to write?

Although pencils made from charcoal have been used for thousands of years, if you'd gone to school in Roman times, about 2000 years ago, you wouldn't have used a pencil. You would have learnt to write by carving the letters in wax tablets with a hard little stick made of bone or metal. If you made a mistake, you would have scraped off the top layer of wax and then had a clean surface to try again.

Pencils as we know them weren't around until about 500 years ago, when a mineral called graphite was discovered in England. The people who found it quickly realised it would be excellent for writing with – much better than a stick of burnt wood or scribbling in wax. Since then, graphite has been used in pencils all over the world.

Wait a minute. If pencils are made of graphite, why do we often call them lead pencils? Well, at the time graphite was discovered, everyone thought it *was* lead, because it looked so similar. It didn't take long for scientists to realise it wasn't, but by then the name had stuck – lead pencils.

Lucky for us our pencils aren't lead, though, because lead is a poisonous metal that can kill you if you get enough of it inside you. That's why you'll sometimes hear people say that it's dangerous to chew your pencil. But relax, it's only harmless graphite! Or else The Word Spy would have died years ago . . .

Pens

What about pens? The early pens that the ancient Romans used were hollow reeds, which they filled with a kind of ink for writing. These were pretty good, but by the Middle Ages, feathers had become the most popular sort of pen. The word 'pen' in fact comes from the Latin word for feather, *penna*. People dipped the bony end of a bird's feather into ink, and scratched out their letters.

It wasn't just a matter of pulling a feather from the tail of your pet budgie though. (Ouch!) You had to pick the right bird. Goose feathers were the most common. Huge goose farms were set up all over Europe to provide feathers for pens, known as quills. Some people even kept their own flock of geese so they could have as many quills as they needed. (They must have been keen writers . . .)

But you could use feathers from any bird, really – eagles, owls, even turkeys – whatever was handy, and depending on what you wanted to write. Back in 1792, the novelist Jane Austen used a very fine crow feather to write a little poem in tiny writing as a gift for a friend. And if you were *very* fussy, the expensive feathers of a swan were meant to be the best of all.

If you find a feather lying in the garden or the playground one day, why not pick it up? Try dipping the bony end into a pot of ink or

paint and write your name on a piece of paper, just to see what it was like.

Hmm, maybe I'll write my next book with a pelican feather – or how about one from a kookaburra?

Fountains and ballpoints

Quills were a step forward but they weren't perfect. They didn't last long and they had to be replaced all the time. Also, you had to keep dipping the end of the quill back in the pot of ink and be very careful not to smudge the page. So people were hard at work to find something better.

It took a while. It wasn't until the 19th century that the metal fountain pen was invented. Inside this pen was a hollow tube called a 'fountain', which you could fill with ink so you didn't keep having to dip it into an inkwell. They were still pretty smudgy to write with though.

Then about a hundred years later, just before World War Two, a man called László Bíró invented something even better. Can you guess what it was? The 'biro', or ballpoint pen. In ballpoint pens, the ink flows down to the tip of the pen, then rolls out under a tiny ball and dries almost immediately. Brilliant!

Now, although many people still love writing with fountain pens, the ballpoint pen has taken over the world. And there are felt-tipped pens, gel pens, all kinds of markers – a universe of pens.

By My Own Hand

Do you know the word 'manuscript'? It usually means the pages of writing an author sends to a publisher to see if they will publish it. These days a manuscript is most often written on a computer and sent electronically. But it wasn't always like that.

The word manuscript comes from two Latin words: *manu* meaning 'by hand', and *scriptus* meaning 'written'. Before the invention of typewriters and computers, everything had to be written first by hand. Even very, very long novels that were hundreds, sometimes thousands, of pages long, were written by hand.

Sometimes museums have manuscripts by famous authors from pre-computer days on display. These manuscripts can look really messy, full of crossings-out, with squiggles and arrows and different coloured pencils – there was no such thing as a delete button then! If an author made a mistake, they had to cross it out and write the new word next to it, or stick a piece of paper on top. Yep, in those days 'cut and paste' really meant cut and paste, with scissors and glue . . .

QWERTY

Around the middle of the 19th century, can you guess what came along that made writing and reading easier? I'll give you a hint. Tap, tap, tap, tap, ping! Tap, tap, tap, tap, ping!

Give up? I'm talking about the invention of the typewriter. Have you ever had a go on one? It will seem very heavy and slow to you, banging away on those keys. But at the time they were invented, people thought they were miraculous. To be able to print out such neat writing, and so easy to read!

Of course, now that computers are everywhere, typewriters are pretty rare. But you see the remains of a typewriter every time you look at your computer keyboard. The first half of that row of letters along the top, QWERTY, is how the letters were laid out on the first Remington typewriters, back in the 1870s.

Nobody knows why the letters are in that

order, although there are a few theories going round. It might have been to try to separate commonly used letters, so the keys of the typewriter wouldn't jam together if you were typing very fast. Or it might have been because with the whole top line, QWERTYUIOP, you can type the word TYPEWRITER. This was certainly handy for salespeople to demonstrate the machines.

QWERTZ, AZERTY, QZERTY . . . PYFGCRL?

The QWERTY keyboard is found all over the world now, although some non-English-speaking countries have adjusted it a little. In Germany they have QWERTZ; in France AZERTY; and in Italy QZERTY. And of course, there are many places in the world where languages are spoken that don't use our alphabet – China, Russia and Greece, for example.

So is QWERTY the best way to put the letters, though? An American psychologist, Dr August Dvorak, didn't think so. He invented a whole new keyboard in the 1930s, which he believed would make typing easier and quicker. He arranged the letters so that the most commonly used ones were in the centre, and the less common ones at the sides. This is what it looks like:

Hmm, so if it's easier to use, why hasn't this keyboard taken over the world? Ah well. It's like sensible spelling, sensible punctuation – there's something very unsensible about human beings sometimes!

My Life as a Cockroach

Even though typewriters are an old technology, some people still like to use them. (Just as some writers still like to write by hand or use fountain pens.) There's even a group of poets known as 'typewriter poets'. They think they write much more interesting poems with their typewriters than they would if they used a computer. (!)

One famous typewriter poet was a cockroach named Archy. He wrote a lot of poems all about the ups and downs of life as a cockroach, and especially about his friendship with Mehitabel the cat. Because he was a cockroach, he had a lot of trouble pushing down the 'shift' key on the typewriter, so his poems are all in the lower case with not much punctuation.

You don't believe me? Don't take my word for it – read on the next page what American journalist Don Marquis had to say about the day he found Archy hard at work in his office, typing.

We came into our room earlier than usual in the morning, and discovered a gigantic cockroach jumping about on the keys. He did not see us, and we watched him . . .

He could not work the capital letters, and he had a great deal of difficulty operating the mechanism that shifts the paper so that a fresh line may be started. We never saw a cockroach work so hard or perspire so freely in all our lives before.

What I like most about Archy's poems is that you have to read them on the page to properly enjoy them – they don't work nearly so well read aloud.

Have a look at this one for yourself and you'll see what I mean:

night after night i have written poetry for you
on your typewriter
and this big brute of a rat who used to be a poet
comes out of his hole when it is done
and reads it and sniffs at it
he is jealous of my poetry
he used to make fun of it when we were both
human
he was a punk poet himself
and after he has read it he sneers
and then he eats it

i wish you would have mehitabel kill that rat
or get a cat that is onto her job
and i will write you a series of poems showing
how things look
to a cockroach

Why don't you try writing a poem yourself about how things look to a cockroach?

Excuse Me, Your Hand Is Shaking

What with typewriters, computers, mobile phones, and all those other gadgets we use, every day we all write by hand less and less. Who knows, maybe one day handwriting itself will become a thing of the past – something weird and old-fashioned that only old people do, like knitting or posting letters.

It's sad, in a way. It's as though the machines have taken over a little piece of ourselves. Like the human voice, your writing is as individual as your fingerprint. It might not look like it, but each person's handwriting contains thousands of complexities that we're not even aware of.

There are specially trained experts in handwriting who can pick up these tiny differences. Things like how heavily or lightly a person writes, where they lift the pen from the page, how thick or thin the lines are, and much more. Some psychologists even think they can tell your personality through your handwriting, and can see if you are suitable for a particular job. Or if you're going to get married, how compatible you are!

There are also experts in handwriting who give evidence in court cases. Their job is to check if a document has been forged by someone trying to copy another person's handwriting or signature. While it's easy to copy the shapes of letters, other things are unconscious and much more difficult to imitate.

These court experts keep a special lookout for something known as the 'tremor of the forger'. A forger will usually write very slowly, trying to copy each letter perfectly. Ah, but the slower you write, the shakier your writing is, even if you can't see the shaky bits without a magnifying glass.

This is not

a forgery...

honest.

Why don't you put your handwriting to the test? You and a friend could each write these sentences on a separate piece of paper:

My handwriting is very difficult to copy.
I bet I can tell who wrote this.

Then try and copy each others' handwriting. Do they look like they were written by the same person? It makes me tremble just thinking about it . . .

The Way of the Ox

There are so many different ways to write, quite apart from what you write with or what you write on. If I asked you what direction you should write in, you'd probably give me a funny look. Across the page, of course!

But sometimes, if you're writing on a very small piece of paper or around a picture, you end out writing in all sorts of directions and shapes. That's how it was done with hieroglyphs, the writing of the ancient Egyptians. They often decided where to put the words or what direction to write in depending on where they thought it looked better.

In English, usually we write words across the page from left to right, starting each line at the left-hand side.

But
why
not
write
down
the
page
like
this?

That's how some Japanese and Chinese languages are written.

?this like backwards write not why Or

That's how people read and write in Arabic and Hebrew.

Or why not write across the page but when going of instead line the of end the to get you back to the beginning just continue on like this?

In ancient Greece, this kind of writing was called *boustrophedon*, which means 'the turning of an ox'. It copied the way people ploughed their fields. When the ox pulling the plough got to the end of the paddock, they made it turn and come back, instead of sending it all the way back to where it started. Often the writing itself was reversed as well, like in a mirror.

It was the best of times,
it was the worst of times,
it was the age of foolishness,
it was the age of wisdom,
it was the

On Reflection

Have you ever tried mirror writing?

That means back to front writing you can only read properly if you hold it up to a mirror.

The famous artist Leonardo da Vinci used to write like this sometimes, perhaps to keep his writing a secret, or perhaps just for fun. Maybe he couldn't help it – there are some people who naturally write like that because it's how their brains see the words.

If it doesn't come naturally to you, though, it's not easy to do. But you can try. (It might be handy to keep a mirror in your pocket in case you forget what it was you actually wrote!)

The Shape of Things

Can you make a picture out of words? That sounds like something impossible, but this way of writing in shapes is very old. People have been doing it for thousands of years, at least since the time of the ancient Greeks. They wrote poems in the shape of things like eggs or wings. Nowadays poems like this are often known as 'concrete poems' or 'picture poems'. The French writer Apollinaire invented another special word for them – 'calligram'. There's one of his calligrams on the next page – it's in French but can you guess what the poem's about?

S
A
LUT
M
O N
D E
DONT
JE SUIS
LA LAN
GUE É
LOQUEN
TE QUESA
BOUCHE
O PARIS
TIRE ET TIRERA
TOU JOURS
AUX A L
LEM ANDS

And here's another one, by Lewis Carroll, from his book *Alice's Adventures in Wonderland.* If you read the poem, I think you'll be able to work out what shape it's in.

Hey, why don't you write your own calligram? You can write it in any shape you like. It could be a birthday cake – or a beetle – or something mysterious, like a shadow. Or even in the shape of a wordy spy?

Fury said to a
mouse, That he
met in the
house,
'Let us
both go to
law: I will
prosecute
you. – Come,
I'll take no
denial; We
must have a
trial: For
really this
morning I've
nothing
to do.'
Said the
mouse to the
cur, 'Such
a trial,
dear Sir,
With
no jury
or judge,
would be
wasting
our
breath.'
'I'll be
judge, I'll
be jury,'
Said
cunning
old Fury:
'I'll
try the
whole
cause,
and
condemn
you
to
death.'

This silly word!
What can it be?
A looking glass
May hold the key . . .

Cockroach

12.

Buried treasure

Finally, At Last, In Conclusion, Before I Go . . .

Well, what a journey we've had together, Spies. It's been a wild and wondrous trip. And as we come to the end of an adventure like this, it seems only right that there is a reward. The best kind of reward – a treasure chest!

You've probably seen the word *thesaurus* on word-processing programs. It's a Greek word originally, meaning 'treasure' and a thesaurus truly is a treasure chest of words. It's a tool you can use when you're stuck writing something. You might, say, be writing a story about a giant ladybird taking over the world, and you think, uh-oh, I've used the word 'giant' too often already. What's another word for giant?

Um. Um. If you're writing on the computer, that's when you would probably hit Shift F7, which will take you to the thesaurus. A thesaurus is a list of similar words (or synonyms). It will tell you that instead of 'giant' you could say:

Huge, massive, enormous, colossal, gigantic, immense, vast, mammoth, immeasurable . . .

Hey, wait a minute! This ladybird is getting way too big! Okay, back to the thesaurus. Some thesauruses will also give you words that have the opposite meaning (antonyms) to the word you've looked up. So for the opposite of giant:

Small, tiny, little, baby, petite, minuscule, diminutive, microscopic, teensy weensy . . .

That's MUCH better.

But thesauruses existed long before computers came along. When The Word Spy was a child, nobody wrote stories on computers – it was all pencils, pens and typewriters then – and so there was no Shift F7. But you could still look things up in a thesaurus.

In those days a thesaurus was a book. The Word Spy had a very special thesaurus that her father gave her, that his father had given him. It was old with thin yellow pages that crackled and smelled strange. This was a copy of the most famous thesaurus in the world, called *Roget's Thesaurus.*

The very first edition of *Roget's Thesaurus* was published in 1852. It was compiled by Dr Peter Roget. (He was English, but his father was Swiss-French, so his surname is pronounced as a French word, *roe-jay.)* Even as a little boy, Dr Roget was always making lists, especially when he was feeling sad. He made lists of all sorts of things – animals, places, things in the garden. Quite a lot of children do this, and adults too.

Dr Roget was so fascinated by words, both their individuality and the connections between them, that he made lists and lists and lists of them, all his life. Until finally he put his word lists together and published them in a book, which he called a 'thesaurus'.

Although there had been books of synonyms published before, Dr Roget's collection was a little different. He thought that every word was unique and irreplaceable, that there were no true synonyms. What he did was take the reader of his thesaurus down a kind of trail of thoughts and associations, as one word led to another through his rather complex and unusual mind.

Just recently, a team of British Word Spies has completed the world's biggest thesaurus, called the *Historical Thesaurus of the Oxford English Dictionary*. It's at least twice as long as Dr Roget's thesaurus, and contains over 600,000 words!

But still, it's *Roget's Thesaurus* that's most likely to be in a library or bookshop. Go on, find a copy for yourself, open it up and let your mind wander.

That's the pleasure of a thesaurus, the way it leads you into places you hadn't thought of. Ah, yes, you will often see a word spy or two (or three or four) flopped happily, gladly, contentedly, gleefully, cheerfully, merrily, joyfully, blissfully, in a corner, flipping over the pages of a handy thesaurus, sinking into the glittering treasure of words . . .

Enjoy your treasure, Spies! You deserve it.

Our code is nearly at the end
The time has come to say goodbye
Which means our final little friend
Must spread her wings and homeward fly . . .

There is a well-known rhyme about me and my house and my children, and even a fire!

Can you guess who I am?

Dear Spies,

This is goodbye, my Spies. So long, farewell, toodleloo, cheerio, adieu adieu. Our voyage is at an end and we are on our way home. But you know what they say:

'The best part of a voyage – by plane,
By ship,
Or train –
Is when the trip is over and you are
Home again!'*

I can hear the whistle blowing. I must hurry. I still haven't packed my bag.

Don't forget my secret message. The instructions are on the next page. I know you can work it out. You're Word Spies, after all!

So long for now. Remember, there are always new and even more remarkable voyages to be made. The words are all yours – speak them, write them, read them, whisper them – and look after them. Keep safe, keep happy and, above all, keep wordy.

Your everlasting friend,

The Word Spy

* From Madeline and the Gypsies by Ludwig Bemelmans

Secret Message

Okay, Spies. Did you manage to find all twelve of the secret words? If you did, you must have quite a zooful by now . . . Anyway, try to keep them all under control! Here's what you need to do.

First, get your list of twelve words, written down in the order of the chapters. Then, write down the very first letter of each word, so that you have twelve letters.

Now, if you look further down the page, you'll see two rows of letters. This is what we spies call a 'substitution code'. It's great for secret messages and it works like this.

Look for each of your twelve letters, one by one, in the alphabet that is on top, and swap each letter for the letter underneath it.

A	B	C	D	E	F	G	H	I	J	K	L	M
M	W	A	I	T	X	N	L	R	V	F	H	E

N	O	P	Q	R	S	T	U	V	W	X	Y	Z
H	V	F	D	S	I	Y	J	G	O	U	E	Q

Use these new letters one by one to fill in the blanks in this sentence. Easy!

Oh, wait. There's one more little trick I've thrown in, just to make it harder. (He he!) I wonder if you'll be able to work out what it is? As my teacher always used to say, don't be backwards in coming forwards! (Or was that don't be forwards in coming backwards?)

!_ _ _ NACUOYOS _ _ _ _ _ _ _ _ _ _
SDROW

Away, away, into the wild sky!
Goodbye, from
Your pal

The Word Spy.

Notes

Notes

Notes

Notes

Notes

PIE
This is not sign language
THEATRE

The PASSAGE of TIME
WELKIN
THESAURUS